GETTING INTO

Law

FOURTH EDITION

Edited by

JUSTINA BURNETT

TROTMAN

Getting into Law
Fourth edition

This fourth edition published in 2002
by Trotman and Company Ltd
2 The Green, Richmond, Surrey TW9 1PL

© Trotman and Company Limited 2002

British Library Cataloguing in Publication Data
A catalogue record for this book is available from the
British Library.

ISBN 0 85660 802 5

Typeset by Mac Style Ltd, Scarborough, N. Yorkshire
Printed and bound in Great Britain
by Creative Print & Design (Wales) Ltd

CONTENTS

**For up-to-date information on law courses go to
www.mpw.co.uk/getintolaw**

PREFACE

Over the past few years the number of applicants for law courses has increased enormously. Furthermore, competition for places on what might be regarded as the 'best' university courses has become more intense as students are becoming increasingly aware that employers are looking carefully at which universities their prospective employees have attended.

During the course of MPW's work advising students on their choice of university course, we have gathered together a huge amount of information on law courses and the legal profession. With the encouragement of Trotman and Company this information has been brought together in this guide.

We are very grateful to all the contributors and we hope that this guide will be of use to anyone considering law as a career.

MPW
February 2002

ACKNOWLEDGEMENTS

The fourth edition of *Getting into Law* has been revised and updated by Justina Burnett, an Employment Solicitor at Lewis Silkin, a medium-sized City law firm. This book is the work of a number of contributors without whose specialist knowledge it would not have been possible. Our thanks go to the following.

Fiona Hindle is an independent careers consultant, who for many years worked as a careers adviser at the University of London Careers Service, providing careers advice to students and graduates in the Faculty of Law at University College London. She specialises in providing full careers consultancy to individuals and employers in the legal profession.

Dr James Holland is the Associate Dean (Academic Studies) in the Faculty of Law at the University of the West of England in Bristol. He is also the co-author of *Learning Legal Rules* published by Blackstone Press.

Julian Webb is the Director of Postgraduate Programmes in the Faculty of Law at the University of the West of England, and has co-written *Learning Legal Rules* with Dr Holland.

Paul Whiteside studied history at both University College London and Queen Mary and Westfield College before completing a Diploma in Law at City University and attending the College of Law. For the past ten years he has been teaching law and social sciences at undergraduate and A-level.

Mike Semple Piggot was Chief Executive of the BPP Law School – one of the independent colleges that is providing postgraduate legal education. He has now set up an innovative virtual law school on the Internet which you can access on www.sppa.co.uk. **Frances Burton** has also provided some valuable comments.

Joanne Hubert works as a legal and financial information researcher.

INTRODUCTION

Unless this book has just slipped off the shelf into your hands and fallen open at this very page, you're probably reading it hoping to pick up some pearls of wisdom on whether or not you should study law. Well, read on… This guide is intended to answer those questions you've always wanted to ask and possibly a few more that have never crossed your mind.

Broadly, there are three sections in this book:

1. A brief description of what solicitors and barristers actually do and how they fit into the scheme of the legal system.
2. Ways in which you can become a solicitor or a barrister, including how to get work experience, and some flow charts to summarise that information.
3. A guide to the vast range of law courses on offer.

Don't be fooled, however, into thinking that *Getting into Law* will do all the work for you so you can put your feet up and watch 'Ally McBeal' on TV!

You will still have to…

■ Revise thoroughly and pass your exams. You can get on to a few university courses with fairly low grades, but those courses might not suit your needs. You'd be better off with higher grades and a wider choice of degree options available to you.

You should also…

■ Do your own research. Talk to your teachers, friends, family, legal practitioners… anyone who might know something about the legal profession. Consider carefully what type of course is appropriate for you. Or, come to that, whether you should even think about studying law in the first place.

AN INTRODUCTION TO THE LEGAL PROFESSION

Your first impression of the legal profession may be via film or television. Go on, admit it – how many of you would secretly like to be Kavanagh, Ally McBeal or one of the glamorous young lawyers living life in the fast lane in 'This Life'. You'll have seen barristers in court robed in wig and gown, confidently destroying a witness with one telling question. Equally, you will be familiar with the sight of the solicitor's office in the high street where wills are drafted or houses conveyed. But what are the differences between barristers and solicitors (other than the barristers' novel dress sense)? And where do lawyers and attorneys come into it?

Well, the legal profession in England and Wales is a split profession – although the split is becoming more blurred as solicitors gain rights of audience (in other words they can address the courts) in civil and criminal courts. Solicitors are like general practitioners in the medical profession. They have direct and continuing contact with their clients and deal with many different aspects of the law, not just those which end up in court.

Barristers are more like consultants or surgeons. Their main function is to wield the scalpel on behalf of clients referred to them by solicitors and they may often only meet their clients on the day of trial. The public are not allowed direct access to barristers, although the Bar Council is proposing that barristers should be allowed to see the public directly in some cases, where they can dispense with the services of a solicitor.

So solicitors and barristers should be seen as operating within a loose team, performing different but necessary roles. The term 'lawyer' is simply a collective term for barristers, solicitors, judges, some civil servants, academic lawyers and even law undergraduates; whereas the word 'attorney' refers to American lawyers and means nothing in English law. We will concentrate on the distinct types of work undertaken by barristers and solicitors.

It is also worth noting, however, that the Scottish legal profession is distinct from that of England and Wales, although there is an equivalent division of the profession between Solicitors and Advocates. Solicitors belong to the Law Society of Scotland; Advocates are collectively referred to as 'The Bar' and belong to the Faculty of Advocates. Legal education, legal traditions, the courts and legal language in Scotland are quite distinct from those used in English Law. So, although there are many similarities between practising north or south of the border, the comments below should be taken as relating specifically to England and Wales only. Some comments on the legal professions in both Scotland and Northern Ireland are on page 25.

WHAT DO LAW GRADUATES DO?

According to the Law Society's Annual Statistical Report 2000, in 1999 there were 19,075 applicants to study law as a first degree in England and Wales, of whom 11,154 were accepted. Of the 9,090 graduates in the summer of 1999, 51 per cent achieved a first or upper second degree result.

In July 2000, 7,793 students enrolled with the Law Society. Of these 60 per cent were women and 22 per cent were drawn from ethnic minorities. There were 7,376 full-time and 1,500 part-time Legal Practice Course (LPC) places available in 2000–2001. Of those who sat the exam in 2000, 77 per cent passed. New traineeships for 1999–2000 increased by about 10 per cent. There were 5,162 solicitors commencing training contracts in 2000–2001.

At present there are almost 13,000 places on law and combined law degree courses in the UK. But there are over 20,000 applicants applying for those places so competition is still acute. After graduation law graduates go into a variety of areas. In 2001 over half went on to further study or training that included the professional legal training courses, the LPC and the Bar Vocational Course (BVC). Fewer than three in ten went straight into work, which included employment as diverse as officer training in the Army, newspaper journalism and marketing. You will also find law graduates in banking, accountancy, management consultancy and the Civil Service. This shows that a law degree, even without further professional training, is a highly marketable degree sought after by many employers.

WOMEN IN THE LEGAL PROFESSION

The number of women law graduates now exceeds the number of men. In August 2001, solicitors with practising certificates totalled 86,603 and the number of women solicitors with practising certificates was 32,395. Although this is less than half, it is a significant increase because since 1990 the total number of solicitors with practising certificates has grown by 51 per cent but the number of women holding practising certificates has more than doubled, having increased by 137 per cent.

The situation at the Bar is somewhat different. The Bar Council confirms that there were 2,761 practising female barristers in England and Wales in 2001, compared with 7,573 males. At the top of the profession the difference is even greater with only 84 female Queen's Counsel (QCs) and 991 male QCs. But the situation seems to vary among different chambers. One young newly qualified female barrister said that women were very well represented at her chambers while others were very male dominated. 'Equality still does not exist at the Bar,' she commented. 'It can be harder to get work of a certain quality. Tenacity is the key. Women need to be more flexible and take the opportunities when they come.' Yet at a firm of City solicitors a trainee noted that in her intake 10 out of 13 were women.

MATURE ENTRANTS TO THE LEGAL PROFESSION

A clear majority of solicitors qualify under the age of 30 and it is not common to qualify once over 40. The situation is the same at the Bar where the success of finding pupillage is greatly reduced for those over the age of 30. However, attitudes of firms and chambers vary considerably. But there is no doubt that if you are a mature candidate, say over 30, you will be at an advantage if you have previous relevant work experience and can demonstrate that you are good with clients. If you are older it is vital that you find out what it would be like to work in a firm of solicitors or chambers to 'test the water'.

On the other hand it can still be useful to do something else after graduating before deciding on the law. One newly qualified barrister said:

> 'After my English Literature degree I did one year's voluntary work abroad then joined the Civil Service Fast Stream for two years before training as a barrister. I think it is very important to go into something else beforehand. Quite a lot of barristers have done other things that can be useful such as teaching.'

CURRENT DEVELOPMENTS

The legal profession is constantly changing, so it is very important you keep up-to-date if you are thinking about a legal career. A good habit is to read the relevant press such as the legal pages of the major newspapers (e.g. *The Times* on a Tuesday). Also look at professional journals such as *The Law Society Gazette* and *The Lawyer*.

- Firms still place much emphasis on good A-level grades in their selection criteria.
- There is some evidence that employers still look at the 'old' universities or what they perceive to be 'good' universities for their trainees. So in some cases students who had to study at regional universities because of financial constraints may be discriminated against.
- More and more students are completing their professional studies part-time mostly due to the lack of financial support.
- The number of students graduating from the LPC without training contracts is reducing. In 2001 there were almost 7,376 students on the full-time LPC, an increase of nearly 300 from 2000. The number of registered two-year training contracts has also increased.
- For the 2000/2001 BVC, 2095 applicants applied for 1,522 full-time and part-time places available on the BVC.
- Growth of paralegals: more paralegals are being recruited to do routine work. This is often seen as a way in for LPC and BVC students.

5

- Technology has overhauled communications by the introduction of e-mail, voicemail, video conferencing as well as the advantages of the Internet.

- Solicitors' firms have become much more international.

THE FUTURE OF TRIAL BY JURY

When most people conjure-up an image of a criminal trial, an integral element will almost certainly be the jury. The principle of trial by jury is rooted in the medieval origins of English law, and it remains a powerful part of the ideology of law. In theory, everyone retains the right to 'trial by one's peers', and jury trial is widely represented as a safeguard against oppressive government or the conviction-minded judge. But what is the reality?

The Process of Jury Trial: One of the greatest causes of concern is the extent to which mis-conviction is the result of deliberate or negligent behaviour by participants in the criminal justice system. Any citizen who is over 18 and under 65, who is not disqualified by virtue of some specific rule, may be required to do jury service. Juries are selected randomly on a local basis from the electoral register. If you are selected, you will be expected to attend your local Crown Court centre with other potential jurors. Each jury must consist of 12 persons.

It is the jury's decision whether or not a person is innocent or guilty on the evidence presented in court. The jury is advised as to the law by a professionally qualified judge, but the decision on the facts is theirs alone. The jury's decision, or 'verdict' is given at the end of the trial, in open court. It must normally be a unanimous one, though in exceptional circumstances, the judge may accept a majority verdict. Where the result is a guilty verdict, then the sentence is determined by the judge, not the jury.

The basic principle in criminal cases is that a defendant will be tried by jury in relation to any offence that is triable in the Crown Court. This court has jurisdiction over a wide range of offences, including the most serious crimes, such as murder, manslaughter, rape and arson, but also many lesser offences against the person or property. Even so, on average, less than 10 per cent of all criminal trials are heard before the Crown Court, with the remainder being dealt with by Justices of the Peace in the Magistrates' Court. Last year the Labour government announced plans to end the right of trial by jury for some defendants. This has been widely criticised, and David Blunkett, the Home Secretary, appears to be having second thoughts about the decision following defeats for the government in the House of Lords. For updates on the progress of the proposed reform, you should access news websites such as those operated by the *BBC* (www.bbc.co.uk), *The Guardian* (www.guardian.co.uk) or *The Independent* (www.independent.co.uk).

WHAT IF I DON'T WANT TO GO INTO THE LAW AFTER MY DEGREE?

Some students study law with no intention of becoming a professional lawyer. The legal knowledge and additional skills gained from a law degree are highly prized and can be applied to a number of jobs. We will look at those skills in more detail in Chapters 4 and 5. But what else can a law graduate do other than law? If you use Clive Anderson or Bill Clinton as your role models the world is your oyster, but here are a few suggestions as to what the rest do...

- **Accountancy**
  Many aspects of accountancy relate to those found in legal practice such as analysing large amounts of technical material, analysing and writing reports and advising clients. Law graduates are often particularly wooed into tax consultancy. Starting salaries are usually high.

- **Administration**
  You need a methodical and precise approach as well as good written and communication skills for this job. Some administrative work is in private industry but most jobs are found in the Civil Service, Local Government, the Health Service, voluntary organisations and Further and Higher Education institutions.

- **Civil Service**
  Interested in policy making and implementation? Then you might think about Civil Service departments with legal responsibilities such

as the Home Office, Inland Revenue, Lord Chancellor's Department and Foreign Office. The Customs and Excise Office and Immigration Service would also value law graduates.

- **Business Management**
  The skills you developed from a law degree will be invaluable in the world of commerce and industry.

- **The City and Finance**
  A number of law graduates are lured into the highly-paid world of investment banking and insurance where your legal background will give you an edge. But beware that competition is extremely tough for these high rewards.

In addition to the above areas law graduates also go into legal publishing, the media, journalism (legal or otherwise), the Police Service, teaching, personnel and a lot more....

Some law graduates choose not to pursue the training to become either a solicitor or a barrister but would still like to do something legally related. They will often move into fields such as paralegal and outdoor clerk work. Paralegals research cases, scan and collate documents whereas outdoor clerks take witness statements on behalf of solicitor's clients and conduct legal research for solicitors, barristers and others plus any administrative work that is required.

For up-to-date information on law courses go to www.mpw.co.uk/getintolaw

For up-to-date information on law courses go to www.mpw.co.uk/getintolaw

WHAT DO SOLICITORS DO?

WHAT'S THE WORK LIKE?

Solicitors usually work in firms. Some work for large companies as part of their in-house legal departments (e.g. the trademarks division) but most are in private practice. According to the Law Society, in August 2001 of the 86,603 solicitors with practising certificates 68,466 were in private practice compared with only 5,831 in commerce and industry. Firms vary in size from two people to hundreds, employing assistant solicitors and trainees as well as the actual partners. The larger the firm the more specialised the individual solicitor's work will be. A small firm in your local high street may undertake a wide range of activities such as drafting wills, conveyancing houses, dealing with divorces and sorting out landlord and tenant issues.

Larger firms have specialist departments like a commercial litigation department, or one covering employment, shipping law or tax. The list of legal specialisms is extensive. The *Chambers and Partners Directory* lists them. But the depth of expertise required can sometimes mean that even large firms only deal with a narrow range of topics.

The main work of solicitors is to act as the first port of call for a client needing help in organising his or her affairs or as a potential litigant (claimant or defendant). If the client needs a will drafting, for instance, the solicitor will interview the client, take all relevant details and advise on the legal implications of a particular course of action. The solicitor would then draft the will or other document and, once all the points have been explained to the client, ensure that all the formalities are completed.

If the client is involved in a dispute the solicitor will often try to resolve the matter by writing to the other party. If the dispute continues the solicitor will then advise on litigation. But the best advice is to avoid litigation at all costs! Their work will then involve taking statements, collecting evidence and preparing the case for trial. In some instances where the amount involved is small the solicitor may represent the client in court. If the client needs help on a criminal law point the solicitor will have to gather the evidence, which may involve a visit to the police station or prison where the client is in custody in order to take instructions.

A solicitor's work can be extremely varied and has the advantage of direct contact with many different types of people. On the other hand, a number of solicitors complain that they deal less with legal points and more with matters like interviewing, counselling, paperwork and office management.

WHAT MAKES A GOOD SOLICITOR?

Solicitors need a vast range of qualities to make them effective. But it is commonly recognised that to get a job you need something to make you stand out from the crowd. Some language and computer skills, as well as an outgoing personality and demonstrating a sense of humour, will give you the edge. You will also need to be someone who is focused and persistent and can provide plenty of evidence of working well with others in a team.

Skills and qualities needed

- Strong academic background
- Good written and verbal communication skills
- Commercial awareness
- Interpersonal skills
- Ability to work under pressure
- Computer skills
- Numeracy
- Time management skills
- Attention to detail
- Ability to take personal responsibility

...and many more.

Working in a large City firm

Sukhraj is a Senior Associate Solicitor with Allen & Overy, a large firm of City solicitors, and has worked for them for over seven years. She went to university in Leicester straight after A-levels and gained an upper second class law degree before taking her professional training at the College of Law in Chester. 'The training contract was not too much of a culture shock after being a student. There were 60 trainees and it was just like going in to a smaller class and not nearly as bad as I thought it would be!' commented Sukhraj. 'We were given loads of training and everyone was very friendly.' During her training she experienced four seats, which are in effect placements in different departments. This included six months in New York in the Banking Department. She confirmed there are now lots of seats abroad although many are still very sought after.

She now works in the Projects Department involving her in project finance plus a lot of banking and international work. 'You need to be willing to take responsibility and be a team player' says Sukhraj, 'but you also need to be able to work on your own'. Her training is on-going as the Law Society stipulates that all solicitors must do at least 16 hours per year to accumulate continuing education points. Training can take the form of lunchtime lectures, full day courses and residential courses. Sukhraj advises that if you are interested in working for a big City firm it is essential you become familiar with the City. 'It's very important to read the quality papers and you need to acquire some commercial "know-how" ' she says. A summer placement is the best way of getting experience. Her hours vary considerably depending on what she is working on but 9am until 7pm is average. 'Working late into the night is very common,' she adds.

CASE STUDY

Working in a provincial firm

Martin is in the second year of his training contract with a firm of solicitors in Brighton. His first degree is in French and he then went on to complete the CPE and the Legal Practice Course before starting his training contract. He studied for his degree in London and says he finds it a refreshing change to be out of the big city but still somewhere where there is a lot going on. 'I enjoyed the LPC' says Martin. 'It was very practical and really tried to teach you the skills needed to do the job. But nothing can prepare you for what it's really like.'

Martin's first few weeks were spent getting used to all the office systems before he started on a formalised training programme covering the two years of his training contract. During that period he will spend time in four seats. 'Trainees have access at all times to a partner or senior solicitor who can help out with any difficulties if required. I'm really enjoying the work and find myself becoming more and more confident all the time.'

Working as an in-house lawyer

Jackie works as an in-house lawyer at Instant Karma, a record company based in London. She was offered the job when working as a trainee with a firm of solicitors in London. 'I have no regrets moving away from private practice. When I moved to my present company it was an enormous transition from my previous firm' says Jackie. 'I suddenly found myself working with a lot of creative people who have a completely different concept of working practices and who sometimes lack professionalism. At Instant Karma I am very much part of the business team and there are no time sheets to complete unlike working for a firm of solicitors'. The actual work she does is very similar, such as arranging production contracts with artists/songwriters, dealing with the copyright issues associated with film soundtracks and compilations, but the atmosphere is totally different from a law firm. 'Here, I am the only lawyer and I have meetings with the Chairman several times a week to discuss new business opportunities.' The best bit about her job is that she gets to go and see the company's artists in action which means gigs around London and some glamorous events like the Brit Awards. Jackie also says: 'there is a purpose to every agreement I draft and negotiate because I see the artist's video and monitor its performance.'

Jackie comments that to succeed as an in-house lawyer, you need to be confident and independent, willing to take total responsibility, to be able to take instructions from a wide variety of people with no legal knowledge and to translate legal issues into layman's terms. Her advice to anyone wanting to work in-house is to train in private practice first. She reckons it is advisable to work at least one year after qualifying before going in-house. She comments that working in-house is often less well paid than working in a law firm. However, in her field, those interested in media law want to work in the industry rather than just being a lawyer. There can be other benefits besides salary, such as a company car and annual bonus. In the music industry reputation is everything. Making and maintaining contacts is crucial for success.

WHO WORKS WHERE?

The vast majority of solicitors work in private practice in a firm of solicitors. But qualified solicitors have a huge choice of organisations in which they could potentially work. The legal profession truly does cater for everyone… from those wishing to specialise in a huge international City-based firm to those preferring to do a 'bit of everything' in a small high street firm.

According to the Law Society in 2001, of the 86,603 qualified solicitors, 68,466 (almost 80 per cent) are working in private practice. Of the rest, the main employers of qualified lawyers are private companies, local government, the Crown Prosecution Service, and advice services.

WHAT IF I WANT TO WORK ABROAD?

Prospects for lawyers wishing to pursue an international career and work abroad have grown greatly in recent years. Opportunities exist to work in the offices of partner firms in other countries, work in the legal department of an international client or even work abroad as part of your training contract. Some big firms have an established international network worldwide. Other opportunities are being created by the increase in overseas firms opening offices in the UK. 'Training with a big international firm gives you so much opportunity for working abroad and travelling,' says one trainee. There are more and more opportunities for lawyers with international experience. If you have spent some time working abroad as a lawyer it is bound to be an asset to your future career prospects. The European Commission also recruits qualified lawyers through open competition but does not recruit trainees. Opportunities for international work at the Bar are very limited.

WHAT DO BARRISTERS DO?

WHAT'S THE WORK LIKE?

One of the complaints about the English legal system is that lawyers are like buses: as soon as one appears a whole gang of them arrives. This impression comes from the fact that solicitors may often employ barristers to give specialist advice or to represent the client in court. So, instead of hiring only one lawyer, you now have at least two on your hands.

We said earlier that the work of barristers compares with consultants or surgeons: they are specialist advocates. Barristers work as individuals and cannot form partnerships with other lawyers. They do form loose groups called 'chambers' where a small number will have their offices in the same building and share the expenses of clerks and common facilities, but these are not firms. Barristers are responsible for their own caseload.

Barristers also come in two forms: junior counsel and senior counsel. This has nothing to do with age, but indicates generally whether a barrister has 'taken silk' or not. This odd phrase relates to the silk used in the gowns worn by senior barristers and it means that the barrister has been appointed 'Queen's Counsel' (QC). A QC is therefore a senior barrister, appearing only in the more important cases in the higher courts, and charging much higher fees.

A solicitor might want to employ a barrister for two main reasons. First, to gain another opinion on a matter of law from a person who is particularly authoritative in that field of law. Second, to represent the client in court where the solicitor is not allowed to or would prefer a specialist advocate to take on the task. When a solicitor asks for a barrister's view on a legal point this is known as seeking 'counsel's opinion'. Where the barrister is asked to undertake litigation work, this is known as 'instructing counsel'. If an opinion is sought the barrister will be sent all the relevant paperwork and will sit down and research that area of law before expressing a view as to the merits of the case. If counsel is instructed to act then, generally speaking, the decision to litigate or defend will have been taken and the barrister will begin to prepare his or her arguments that they will later argue in court. So most of the barrister's work will be centred on legal disputes. The barrister acts like the old medieval champion: stepping in to fight in the place of the client.

There are over 9,000 barristers in independent practice in England and Wales. They specialise in a wide variety of areas including Building and Construction, Commercial Company, Criminal, Employment, Personal Injury, Liquidation, Taxation, Property and many more. Barristers also work for the Crown Prosecution Service (CPS), the Government Legal Service (GLS) and the Inner London Magistrates Courts.

Barristers' work usually comes through the referral of a solicitor. Sometimes, barristers provide their services free of charge such as through the Free Representation Units or the Bar Pro Bono Unit. In some humanitarian cases pro bono work has also been carried out.

There has recently been a great increase in the size of the Bar. This has meant that the number of Chambers has also increased. Most barristers practise from London but nearly 3,000 barristers practise from other large cities in the UK as well as some small towns outside London.

WHAT MAKES A GOOD BARRISTER?

'You need to have utter confidence in what you are doing – or at least appear to,' says one newly qualified young barrister. 'You are absolutely vulnerable to the whims of the solicitor. You put your soul into a piece of work and you need to be robust so as not to take it too personally.' The key skill for a barrister is the ability to persuade, so strong communication skills are at the top of the list. To be an effective barrister you also need to be interested in business and be commercially aware.

Skills and qualities needed

- Good academic ability
- Flexibility and ability to adapt

- Written and verbal communication skills
- Numeracy
- Interpersonal skills
- Computer skills
- Professional conduct
- Independence
- Confidence
- Commercial awareness
- Meticulous
- A lot of drive

... and many more.

WHO WORKS WHERE?

Most barristers are in independent practice (approximately 80 per cent). The Crown Prosecution Service employs around 5 per cent of barristers, and others work for the government legal service, and for magistrates' courts.

CASE STUDY

The experienced barrister

Paul is an experienced barrister working from chambers in London since 1985. Most of his work is with insurers, giving them advice on whether or not they should meet a claim. He deals a lot with recovery work and employers' liability. 'It is very important to build up your reputation. This often starts with your clerk who will recommend you to do a piece of work from solicitors. After that you'll tend to build up your reputation word-of-mouth,' says Paul. 'Your task in Court is to persuade the tribunal, so good communication skills are vitally important. You also need to communicate effectively with your own clients. A good grasp of the law and the enthusiasm to carry on learning is necessary.' A lot of stamina is required to be a barrister as the job is very hard work, often requiring you to work more than 10-hour days, sometimes six or seven days a week. 'Working from 6am until midnight is common, especially on a long case which can go on for weeks on end,' says Paul.

Because it is a tough profession Paul advises that you should give it serious thought. 'It's a very enjoyable profession. For people who like to be independent and work for themselves – it's the ideal profession. But you need to be able to work on your own initiative and find a way of managing the profession and your life so that it does not entirely dominate your life'. He says you need a minimum 2(i) degree and advises you to do a mini-pupillage, preferably at places you plan to apply for pupillage.

**For up-to-date information on law courses go to
www.mpw.co.uk/getintolaw**

HOW TO BECOME A SOLICITOR

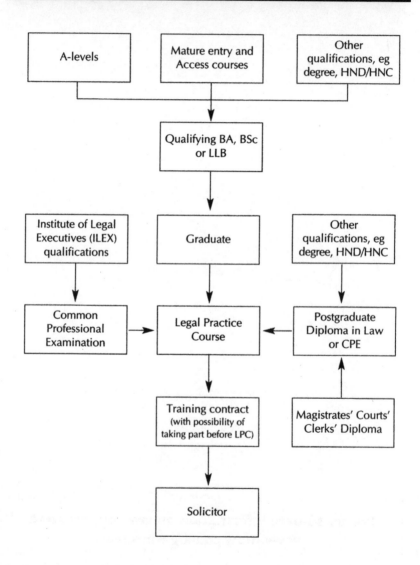

Main routes to qualifying as a solicitor

MAIN ROUTES TO QUALIFYING AS A SOLICITOR

There are a number of routes into the legal profession as you can see from the diagram on page 18.

A-levels and equivalents

Nearly all A-level subjects are acceptable. Legal study is something of a cross between the arts and sciences and so a combination of subjects would prove a very good grounding. Contrary to popular belief, taking law at A-level or AS-level is not an advantage for a law degree. It is also quite common for general studies to be discounted by some universities. You'll need to pay particular attention to each Law School's entrance requirements. Also note that an A-level or AS-level modern language could be an advantage if you apply for a job with one of the big law firms.

But you will need to have a strong academic background. University admissions tutors and subsequently firms of solicitors will look for three good A-level grades (or equivalent) and possibly a high grade at AS-level as part of their selection criteria. Specific grades will vary but the 'old' universities and the big firms will certainly look for and get candidates with mostly grades A and B.

Access courses

A-levels need not be the only entry pathway. Many universities now encourage mature students (who may have missed out on the opportunity to enter Higher Education) to apply for entry on to degree courses, taking into account their work experience and commitment as part of the entry criteria. There are now Access courses in colleges around the country that specifically prepare mature students for higher education. Mature students now constitute a third of the intake in many university law faculties. The difficulties they face are that they are not as accustomed to study as the young A-level entrant, but they possess an advantage in that law is concerned with the everyday practical problems which they may well have faced.

The Law degree

There are now many variations in the design of law degrees. You will find courses concentrating on traditional law subjects, or ones involving a high percentage of European or comparative law, or joint degrees (e.g. Law and Politics). You must choose one that suits your interests and possible career path. But if you are going to pursue a career as a solicitor you will need to ensure that the degree is a qualifying degree. This is one recognised by the Law Society as containing the subjects you must study for your degree. Most LLB courses will be qualifying degrees but you need to check first. Contact the Law Society for a list of qualifying law degrees and see the table at the end of this chapter.

Many courses allow you to choose optional subjects that allow some specialism within your course. These options may even extend to non-law subjects such as forensic science or accounts or hybrids such as criminology.

During a normal three-year course students would be expected to have at least 50 per cent of their workload studying law. The seven foundation subjects on a law degree are contract, tort, equity and trusts, criminal law, property law, public law and European Union law. It is important to gain a minimum upper second degree, as it is very difficult to get a training contract with a lower degree.

Exempting law degrees

Currently, only the University of Northumbria at Newcastle runs this approved law degree. The degree integrates the LLB with the LPC and lasts for four years. Clearly, it would not be appropriate for a student wishing to pursue a career at the Bar or one who is undecided as to which career option to pursue.

The CPE/Diploma in Law

If you take a degree subject other than law you can still pursue a legal career. But you will need to take a course which concentrates on the seven foundations of legal knowledge and one other area of legal studies. These are the same subjects which are demanded in a 'Qualifying' law degree. Courses known as the Common Professional Examination or a Postgraduate Diploma in Law are offered by a number of universities. Both courses cost approximately £2,500 to £3,550 and are intensive and usually last one academic year full-time or two years part-time. See the table at the end of this chapter for a list of institutions which provide CPE/PGDL courses.

Applying for a place on a CPE/Diploma course is done via the CPE Applications Board in Guildford. Application forms are available from November and the closing date is 15 February.

The Non-Graduate (ILEX) route

If you do not possess a degree and work in legal employment, you can qualify as a solicitor via the Institute of Legal Executives (ILEX). It is a lengthy and demanding process and ILEX require that you enter and maintain legal employment approved by ILEX.

The Legal Practice course

The LPC is the professional stage of training for prospective solicitors. Most LPC courses have a commercial bias and are very intensive and hard work. The average first-time national pass rate is just under 70 per cent. There are around 30 institutions validated by the Law Society to provide the LPC. On every LPC course six skills areas are taught. These are practical legal research, writing and drafting, interviewing, advising, and advocacy. There are also three main compulsory subjects: business law and practice, conveyancing, and litigation. Assessment is normally a combination of examination and coursework. See the table at the end of this chapter for a list of providers.

CASE STUDY

Legal Practice course student

Mark was always very clear about his career aspirations, but decided that in order to have the option of specialising in intellectual property he needed to complete a science degree as some of the work can involve patents and scientific know-how. He studied Chemistry at Imperial College and spent two years in London and two in Paris, where he did research and studied some French literature. Having planned

21

with precision, Mark applied to do his CPE at The College of Law in London. 'I wanted to move back to London after Paris and wanted to be at the College, because it has a reputation for quality courses and is well recognised by leading firms. I had already started doing vacation placements at various firms and knew that although I enjoyed the research, long term, I wanted to work in a profession more orientated around people.'

Mark found the CPE very fast paced and practical, which is excellent for a scientist who has always dealt with the practical applications of his experiments. 'CPE students do miss out a little on discussing the implication of law, but the practical aspects are great and really prepare you for life in a law firm.' Mark had always been part of a debating team, all through school and university and when he arrived at the College, he was keen to help give the debating team a boost. 'Debating introduces you to the skills of presenting your case in a logical way and in public. All solicitors need these skills as they have to talk to clients, think on their feet and justify their actions in an ordered and coherent way.'

Training contract

A student who has passed the LPC cannot yet be called a solicitor. To gain this title you will need to undertake a 'training contract' in a firm of solicitors. The training contract will last two years. During that time you will be instructed in various aspects of legal work, spending time in each department within the firm. The crunch comes after the LPC when potential solicitors fight for positions as trainee solicitors. Competition still exists to secure a training contract so although you might get onto an LPC with a lower second class degree or less your chances of getting a training contract will be greatly reduced.

Solicitor advocates

The Access to Justice Act 1999 introduced major amendments to the Courts and Legal Services Act 1990 which grant solicitors the right to appear in all courts in all proceedings with effect from 31 July 2000. Solicitors may appear before the County Court, Magistrates Court, and before Tribunals. If solicitors obtain further advocacy training and qualification from the Law Society they may appear before the Crown Court, High Court, Court of Appeal and the House of Lords. Solicitors will not, however, be allowed to wear the traditional wig worn by barristers. Barristers have been worried for some time about losing business in an already shrinking litigation market to solicitor advocates, but as yet there are few signs that this is happening.

FUNDING

Gaining a professional qualification takes time and costs a lot of money. At the time of writing, fees alone for the LPC are at least £7,500 at most institutions notwithstanding the costs for accommodation and maintenance. The Law Society and the Bar are pressing the Government for a revision of existing policy on financial support for law students.

You may be able to secure financial assistance for your professional training from one or more of the following sources:

Local Authority Grants – Contact your Local Education Authority for information. The CPE, Postgraduate Diploma in Law and LPC fall into the category of discretionary awards. Funds for these awards are very limited and it is advisable to apply as soon as possible. Check with your Local Authority for application dates.

Bank Loans – A number of banks offer loans at favourable rates. The National Westminster Bank – Trainee Solicitors' Group Loan Scheme – offers LPC students who have secured a training contract special loan facilities (call 08457 555 000 for more information). HSBC (call 0800 881 155), Royal Bank of Scotland (call 0131 523 2631) and Barclays Bank (call 020 7699 5000) offer similar loans.

Career Development Loans – These are operated on behalf of the Department for Education and Skills (DfES) by four high street banks: Barclays, Clydesdale, the Co-operative and the Royal Bank of Scotland. The maximum loan is £8,000 if the qualifying criteria are met. For a free booklet on Career Development Loans contact your local Job Centre or one of the participating banks.

Charities and Grant-making Trusts – Refer to the books *The Charities Digest* and *The Directory of Grant-Making Trusts*.

Law Society Bursary Scheme – The funds available are limited and applications are competitive. Contact the Legal Education Department at the Law Society for information.

College Access Funds – Available to postgraduate students at universities. Contact the Student Services for information.

Ethnic Minority Students – A limited number of scholarships are available for the LPC for members of ethnic minority groups. Contact the Ethnic Minorities Office at the Law Society for information.

Sponsorship – a number of firms will sponsor students to whom they have offered a training contract for the LPC and/or CPE. The larger commercial firms may even pay maintenance costs. Further information is available from *The Lawyer – Student Special Supplement*. Copies are usually kept in university careers services.

CASE STUDY

Working as a trainee solicitor

Karen is a trainee at Lewis Silkin, a medium-sized law firm based in the City of London renowned for its specialist areas of expertise, in particular employment, advertising and social housing. Karen completed A-levels in English language, law, mathematics and general studies. She obtained three A grades and a B grade. Karen went straight to Bristol University where she read law. In her first year she read tort, criminal, public and property law. In her second she chose jurisprudence, contract, property, trusts and European law. In her third she elected to do medicine, law and ethics, intellectual property, revenue law, and gender and the law. She obtained a 2.1.

Karen seemed clear from the start that she wanted to be a solicitor. She comments: 'I wanted to be able to deal with clients from the beginning of a case and because of the possibilities for solicitor advocates nowadays it didn't seem to be closing any doors. I also dislike the stuffy traditions of the bar.' Karen obtained a distinction on the LPC.

Karen also made sure that she gained work experience through summer work placements. 'After my second year at University I spent an intensive summer working for White and Case for two weeks, Barlow Lyde and Gilbert for two weeks, Olswang for three weeks and Mirror Group Newspapers (in-house legal department) for one week.'

Karen is in her first seat in the employment department at Lewis Silkin. She hopes to proceed to corporate as her next seat. A typical day in the employment department could involve her attending a tribunal, preparing documents for a tribunal hearing, interviewing a witness and drafting the witness statement, attending conference with counsel or assisting in negotiating a settlement or reviewing contractual documents, for example, a contract of employment.

There are six trainees per year (that is, 12 at any one time) at Lewis Silkin. The favoured seats for a training contract are corporate, employment, litigation and intellectual property. In addition to the Professional Skills Course (PSC), Lewis Silkin conducts in-house training for its trainees.

There is a good induction programme at Lewis Silkin and a comprehensive system of support so there is always someone to help you when you need it. However, because of the intense competition for training contracts Karen thinks you really need something to help you stand out. 'Being outgoing, having a sense of humour, and language and computer skills will give you the edge,' she says. 'My legal experience also helped enormously'. She advises, 'You must be very committed before going to Law School as costs are great unless you are sponsored. Be focused and persistent.'

Professional Skills Course (PSC)

During your training contract you will have to complete the PSC before you can be admitted as a solicitor. The course is divided into three compulsory courses: advocacy and communications skills, finance and business skills, client care and professional standards. There are a number of Law Society accredited PSC providers.

QUALIFYING AS A SOLICITOR IN SCOTLAND

The legal system in Scotland differs from that of England and Wales and Northern Ireland. It is not possible to go into great detail in this book but here is a summary.

It is possible to study a Bachelor of Law degree (LLB) at five Scottish universities. The LLB is offered as an Ordinary Degree over three years or an Honours Degree over four years. Admission requirements to all LLB degrees are high. After completion of the LLB Degree all intending solicitors are required to take the Diploma in Legal Practice which lasts seven months. The course has been designed to teach the practical knowledge and skills necessary for the working life of a solicitor. After successful completion of the Degree and Diploma, you need to serve a two-year post-Diploma training contract with a practising solicitor in Scotland. For further information contact The Law Society of Scotland. See 'Finding out more' at the end of this book for the address.

QUALIFYING AS A SOLICITOR IN NORTHERN IRELAND

Again, it is not possible to go into detail but here is a summary.

Law graduates who wish to practise in Northern Ireland should apply for the one-year Vocational Certificate course at Queen's University, Belfast. Non-law graduates must complete the two-year Bachelor of Legal Science Studies at the same university before taking the Vocational Certificate course. For further information contact The Law Society of Northern Ireland. See 'Finding out more' at the end of this book for the address.

QUALIFYING LAW DEGREES

The following tables list the institutions offering full-time law degrees, giving the qualification gained and title of the degree. It is essential that you check the current prospectuses for full details of the course to which you plan to apply.

England and Wales

Universities	Degree awarded	Title of degree
Aberystwyth	LB	Law
(University College of Wales)	LLB	Law & European Language
01970 623 111	BSc (Econ)	Law & Economics
www.aber.ac.uk	BSc (Econ)	Law & Political Science
	BSc (Econ)	Law & Accounting & Finance
	BSc (Econ)	Law and Business Studies
	BA	Law
	BA	Law with European Languages
Anglia Polytechnic	LLB	Law
University	BA	Combined Honours
01245 493 131		
www.apu.ac.uk		
Aston University	BSc	Managerial & Admin Studies
(Birmingham)		(Legal Studies)
0121 359 3611		
www.aston.ac.uk		
University of Central	LLB	Law (including language
England in Birmingham		options)
0121 331 5000	BA	Law with Politics
www.uce.ac.uk	LLB	Law with Minor studies
Birmingham University	LLB	Law
0121 414 3344	LLB	Law with French
www.bham.ac.uk	LLB	Law & Business Studies
	LLB	Law & Politics
	LLB	Law with European Law
Bournemouth University	LLB	Business Law (Sandwich)
01202 595 187	LLB	Law & Taxation
www.bournemouth.ac.uk		
University of the West	LLB	Law
of England in Bristol	LLB	European Law & Languages
0117 965 6261	LLB	Law & Comparative
www.uwe.ac.uk		European Legal Studies
University of Bristol	BSc	Chemistry and Law
0117 928 7453	LLB	European Legal Studies
www.bris.ac.uk	LLB	Law
	LLB	Law & French
	LLB	Law & German

Universities	Degree awarded	Title of degree
University of Brighton 01273 642 570 www.bton.ac.uk	BA	Law with Accountancy
Brunel University (University of West London) 01895 274 000 www.brunel.ac.uk	LLB LLB LLB BSc	Business & Finance Law (incl. Sandwich) Law French/German Economic & Law (incl. Sandwich)
Buckingham University 01280 814 080 www.buckingham.ac.uk	LLB LLB LLB LLB	Law (2 years duration) European Studies (2 years duration) Law, Biology & Environment (2 years duration) Politics & Law (2 years duration)
Cambridge University 01223 337 733 www.cam.ac.uk	BA	Law Tripos
Cardiff University 029 2087 4348 www.cf.ac.uk/claws	LLB LLB LLB LLB LLB LLB LLB LLB LLB	Law Law & French Law & German Law & Italian Law & Japanese Law & Spanish Law & Sociology Law & Politics Law & Criminology
City University 020 7040 8308 www.city.ac.uk	LLB	Law
Coventry University 01203 631 313 www.coventry.ac.uk	LLB LLB LLB LLB	Legal Studies Business Law Criminal Justice with English European Law with a language
De Montfort University 01162 551 551 www.dmu.ac.uk	LLB LLB LLB BA BSc	Law Law with French Law with German Law Combined Studies (qualifying route only)

Universities	Degree awarded	Title of degree
University of Derby 01332 622 222 www.derby.ac.uk	LLB	Law
Dundee University 01382 344 461 www.dundee.ac.uk	LLB LLB LLB LLB	English Law Law & Accountancy Law with French Law with German (in all cases the courses on the English Law stream must be taken)
Durham University 0191 374 2000 www.dur.ac.uk	LLB BA BA BA LLB	Law Law & Economics Law & Politics Law & Sociology European Legal Studies
East Anglia University 01603 592 520 www.uea.ac.uk	LLB LLB LLB LLB LLB	Law Law with German Law & Language Law with French Law & Language Law with European Legal Systems Law with American Legal Studies
University of East London 020 8223 3000 www.uel.ac.uk	LLB BA	Law Law (Major)
University of Essex 01206 873 333 www.essex.ac.uk	LLB LLB LLB LLB LLB LLB LLB LLB	Law English & European Laws European Law with Sociology Law & Philosophy English & French Law/Maitrise en Droit University of Paris X (Nanterre) Law and Human Rights Law and Politics
Exeter University 01392 263 263 www.ex.ac.uk	LLB LLB BA (Law) BA (Law)	Law European Law Law & Society Chemistry & Law

Universities	Degree awarded	Title of degree
University of Glamorgan 01443 480 480 www.glam.ac.uk	LLB	Law
University of Greenwich 020 8316 8000 www.gre.ac.uk	LLB BA	Law Law
University of Hertfordshire 01707 284 000 www.herts.ac.uk	LLB LLB BSc BA BA	Law Law (Accelerated Programme – 2 years duration) Combined Studies Social Science Business Studies (Law Major)
University of Huddersfield 01484 422 288 www.hud.ac.uk	LLB LLB BA	Law Business Law Law and Accountancy
Hull University 01482 46311 www.hull.ac.uk	LLB LLB LLB LLB LB LLB	Law Law with French Law with German Law with Sociology Law with Philosophy Law with Politics
Keele University 01782 621 111 www.keele.ac.uk	BA	Law & another subject

* All degrees at the University of Keele are Joint Honours; where a degree is designated as Law this will constitute a Qualifying Law Degree.

Kent University (Canterbury) 01227 764 000 www.ukc.ac.uk	LLB LLB LLB LLB LLB LLB BA	Law English & French Law English & German Law English & Italian Law English & Spanish Law European Legal Studies Combined Studies
Kingston University 020 8547 2000 www.king.ac.uk	LLB BA LLB LLB	Law Accounting & Law Law with French Law with German

Universities	Degree awarded	Title of degree
University of Central Lancashire	LLB	Law
01772 201 201	LLB	Law with French
www.uclan.ac.uk	LLB	Law & German
	BA	Law (Combined Honours)
	BSc	Law (Combined Honours)
Lancaster University	LLB	Law
01524 65201	LLB	European Legal Studies
www.lancs.ac.uk		
Leeds Metropolitan University	LLB	Law
0113 283 2600	BA	Law with IT
www.lmu.ac.uk		
Leeds University	LLB	Law
0113 243 1751	LLB	English Law with a European
www.leeds.ac.uk		Law
	LLB	Law & Chinese Studies
	LLB	Law & Japanese Studies
	LLB	Law & French Studies
Leicester University	LLB	Law
0116 252 2363	LLB	Law with French Law &
www.le.ac.uk		Language
	LLB	European Union
	BA	Economics and Law
University of Lincolnshire and Humberside 01482 440 550 www.ulh.ac.uk	BA	Law & another subject

*All BA Law degrees at the University of Humberside and Lincolnshire are Law Major and are recognised Qualifying Law Degrees.

Universities	Degree awarded	Title of degree
Liverpool John Moores University 0151 231 2121 cwis.livjm.ac.uk	LLB	Law
Liverpool University	LLB	Law
0151 794 2000	LLB	Law & French
www.liv.ac.uk	LLB	Law & German
London Guildhall University	LLB	Law
020 7320 1000	LLB	Business Law
www.lgu.ac.uk	BA	Legal Studies
	BA	Law and another discipline

Universities	Degree awarded	Title of degree
London School of Economics	LLB	Law
& Political Science	LLB	Law with German
020 7955 7007	LLB	Law with French
www.lse.ac.uk	LLB	Law & Anthropology
	LLB	Law & Government
King's College	LLB	Law
020 7836 5454	LLB	English & French Law
www.kcl.ac.uk	LLB	Law with German Law
	LLB	European Legal Studies
School of Oriental & African	LLB	Law
Studies	BA	Law & another discipline
020 7367 2388	BA	Law & a language
www.soas.ac.uk		
Queen Mary & Westfield	LLB	Law
College	LLB	English & European Law
020 7882 555	LLB	Law with German Language
www.qmw.ac.uk	BA	Law & Economics
	BA	Law & Politics
	BA	Law & German
University College	LLB	Law
020 7387 7050	LLB	Law with Advances Studies
www.ucl.ac.uk	LLB	Law with French Law
	LLB	Law with German Law
	LLB	Law with Italian Law
University of Luton	LLB	Law
01582 734 111	BA	Law with French
www.luton.ac.uk		
Manchester Metropolitan	LLB	Law
University	LLB	English & French Law
0161 275 2000	BA	Accounting and Law
www.man.ac.uk	BA	Government & Law
Middlesex University	LB	Law
020 8362 5000	BA	Law Major
www.mdx.ac.uk		
Newcastle upon Tyne	LLB	Law
University	BA	Accounting & Law
0191 222 6000	BA	Law with French
www.ncl.ac.uk		

Universities	Degree awarded	Title of degree
University of North London 020 7607 2789 www.uni.ac.uk	LLB	Law
University of Northumbria at Newcastle 0191 232 6002 www.unn.ac.uk	LLB LLB	Law French & English Law
Nottingham Trent University 0115 941 8418 www.ntu.ac.uk	LLB LLB LLB LLB	Law Law (Sandwich) Europe with French Europe with German
Nottingham University 0115 951 7500 www.nott.ac.uk	LLB BA BA LLB/BA LLB/BA BA BA LLB/BA LLB/BA BA	Law Law Law & Politics Law with American Law Law with European Law Law with American Law & Politics Law with European Law & Politics Law with South East Asian Law Law with Chinese Law Law with Chinese Law & Politics
Oxford Brookes University 01865 741 111 www.brookes.ac.uk	LLB BA	Law Law & another discipline
Oxford University 01865 270 000 www.ox.ac.uk	BA	Jurisprudence
University of Plymouth 01752 600 600 www.plym.ac.uk	LLB	Law
Queen's University, Belfast 028 90273452 www.qub.ac.uk	LLB LLB LLB BSc	Law Law & Accounting Common & Civil Law with French Legal Science Degree
Reading University 0118 987 5123 www.rdg.ac.uk	LLB LLB LLB	Law Law with French Law Law with Legal Studies in Europe

Universities	Degree awarded	Title of degree
Sheffield Hallam University	LLB	Law
0114 225 5555	LLB	Maitrise en Droit Francais
www.shu.ac.uk	BA	Law & Criminology
Sheffield University	LLB	Law
0114 222 6771	BA	Law
www.shef.ac.uk	BA	Law & Criminology
	BA	Law with French
	BA	Law with German
	BA	Law with Spanish
Southampton University	LLB	Law
023 8059 5000	BSc	Accounting & Law
www.soton.ac.uk	BSc	Politics & Law
South Bank University	LLB	Law
020 7928 8989	LLB	Law & Accounting
www.sbu.ac.uk	BA/BSc (Hons)	Law & Business Information Technology
	BA/BSc (Hons)	Law & Economics
	BA/BSc (Hons)	Law & English Studies
	BA/BSc (Hons)	Law & French
	BA/BSc (Hons)	Law & Psychology
	BA/BSc (Hons)	Law & Spanish (ab initio)
	BA/BSc (Hons)	Law & German (Post A-Level)
	BA/BSc (Hons)	Law & Human Resource Management
	BA/BSc (Hons)	Law & Management
	BA/BSc (Hons)	Law & Politics
	BA/BSc (Hons)	Law & Social Policy
	BA/BSc (Hons)	Law & Sociology
	BA/BSc (Hons)	Law & Tourism Studies
Staffordshire University	LLB	Law
01782 294 550	LLB	Law & Language
www.staffs.ac.uk	LLB	Law & Accounting
	BA	Modern Studies
	BA	Law and another discipline
University of Sunderland	LLB	Law
0191 515 2319	LLB	Law & Business
www.sund.ac.uk	LLB	Law & Psychology

Universities	Degree awarded	Title of degree
Surrey University 01483 300 800 www.surrey.ac.uk	BSc BSc BSc LLB LLB LLB LLB	French & Law German & Law Russian & Law Law & European Studies Law & French Law & German Law & Russian
Sussex University 01273 606 755 www.susx.ac.uk	LLB LLB LLB/BA BA BA BA	Law European Commercial Law Law with French; Law with German; Law with Italian; Law with Spanish; Law with Russian Law with North American Studies Law and Economics Law with History
University of Wales, Swansea 01792 481 000 www.swan.ac.uk	LLB LLB	Law Law with Business Studies, Language & Politics
University of Teeside 01642 218 121	LLB	Law
Thames Valley University 020 8579 5000 www.tvu.ac.uk	LLB BA	Law Criminal Justice (2001/2002 only)
Warwick University 01203 523 523 www.csv.warwick.ac.uk	LLB LLB LLB LLB	Law European Legal Studies Law & Languages Commercial Law
University of Westminster 020 7911 5000 www.wmin.ac.uk	LLB LLB LLB LLB	Law European Legal Studies Law & Languages Commercial Law
University of Wolverhampton 01902 321 999 www.wlv.ac.uk	LLB BA	Law Law (Major)

Scotland

Universities	Degree awarded	Title of degree
University of Aberdeen 01224 272000 www.abdn.ac.uk.	LLB	Law
University of Dundee 01382 223 181 www.dundee.ac.uk.	LLB	Law
University of Edinburgh 0131 650 1000 www.ed.ac.uk.	LLB	Law
University of Glasgow 0141 339 8855 www.gla.ac.uk	LLB	Law
University of Strathclyde 0141 553 4400 www.strath.ac.uk.	LLB	Law

Northern Ireland

Universities	Degree awarded	Title of degree
Queen's University, Belfast 028 9024 5133 www.qub.ac.uk	LLB LLB LLB LLB LLB	Law Law with Politics Law with Accounting Law with French Law with Hispanic Studies
University of Ulster 01265 44141 www.ulst.ac.uk	BA BA	Government & Law Law & Economics

Ireland

Universities	Degree awarded	Title of degree
University College, Cork 00 353 21 902 532	BCL BCL	Law French & German
Trinity College, Dublin 00 3531 677 2941	LLB	Law
University College, Dublin 00 3531 706 777	BCL	Law

Universities	Degree awarded	Title of degree
University College, Galway 00 353 91 524 411	LLB	Law
University of Limerick 00 353 61 202 344	LLB	Law

Colleges

England and Wales	Degree awarded	Title of degree
Bradford College (awarded by University of Bradford) 01274 753 111	LLB	Law
Buckingham Chilterns University College 01494 522 141	LLB BA	Law Law Major
Mid Kent College (awarded by University of Kent) 01632 830 633	BA BA BA BA BA	Law & Business Studies Law & European Studies Law & Politics Law & Psychology Law & Social Science
University College Northampton 01604 735 500	LLB	Law
Southampton Institute of Higher Education 023 8031 9000	LLB BA	Law Business & Law
Swansea Institute of Higher Education (awarded by University of Wales) 01792 481 000	LLB LLB	Law Law

Part-time Degrees

England and Wales	Degree awarded	Title of degree
Birkbeck College, University of London 020 7631 6570	LLB	Part-time

University of Central England at Birmingham 0121 331 5000	LLB	Part-time
University of the West of England at Bristol 0117 965 6261	LLB	Part-time
Buckingham University 01280 814 080	LLB	Part-time
Coventry University 024 7663 1313	LLB	Part-time
De Montford University 0116 255 1551	LLB	Part-time
University of Derby 01332 622 222	LLB	Part-time
University of East London 020 8590 7722	LLB	Part-time
University of Glamorgan 01443 480 480	LLB	Part-time
University of Hertfordshire 01707 284 000	LLB	Part-time
University of Huddersfield 01484 422 288	LLB	Part-time
Hull University 01482 46311	LLB	Part-time
Kingston University 020 8547 2000	LLB	Part-time (Combined Studies)
University of Central Lancashire 01772 201 201	LLB	Part-time
Leeds Metropolitan University 0113 283 2600	LLB	Part-time
Liverpool John Moores University 0151 231 2121	LLB	Part-time
London Guildhall University 020 7320 1000	LLB	Part-time

England and Wales	Degree awarded	Title of degree
University of Luton 01582 734 111 e-mail: law@luton.ac.uk	LLB	Part-time
Manchester Metropolitan University 0161 247 2000	LLB	Part-time, evenings
University of North London 020 7862 8360/1/2	LLB	Part-time
University of Northumbria at Newcastle 0191 232 6002	LLB	Part-time or part-time distance learning
Nottingham Trent University 0115 951 7500 www.ntu.ac.uk	LLB	Part-time or part-time distance learning
Oxford Brookes 01865 741 111 www.brookes.ac.uk	LLB	Part-time
Sheffield Hallam University 0114 272 0911	LLB	Part-time
South Bank University 020 7928 8989	LLB	Part-time
Staffordshire University 01782 744 531	LLB	Part-time
University of Teeside 01642 218 121	LLB	Part-time
Thames Valley University 020 8579 5000	LLB BA	Part-time Criminal Justice part-time
University of Westminster 020 7911 5000	LLB	Part-time
University of Wolverhampton 01902 321 999 www.wlv.ac.uk	LLB	Part-time

Degrees by External Studies

	Degree awarded	Title of degree
University of London 020 7862 8360/1/2	LLB LLB	Part-time or part-time distance learning
The Open University 01908 858 585 http://oubs.open.ac.uk/law	LLB	Law (in conjunction with College of Law)

Exempting Law Degrees

	Degree awarded	Title of degree
University of Northumbria at Newcastle 0191 232 6002 www.unn.ac.uk	LLB	Integrating the Legal Practice Course

INSTITUTIONS PROVIDING CPE/PGDL COURSES

ANGLIA POLYTECHNIC UNIVERSITY
(full-time/part-time)
Anglia Polytechnic University, Bishop Hall Lane, Chelmsford, Essex
CM1 1SQ. Tel: 01245 493131

UNIVERSITY OF BIRMINGHAM(full-time)
Law Division, PO Box 363, Birmingham B15 2TT. Tel: 0121 414 6432

BOURNEMOUTH UNIVERSITY(full-time/part-time)
Dorset House, Talbot Campus, Fern Barrow, Poole, Dorset BH12 5BB.
Tel: 01202 595187
BPP LAW SCHOOL (full-time)
67–69 Lincoln's Inn Fields, London WC2A 3JB. Tel: 020 7430 2304

UNIVERSITY OF BRIGHTON (part-time)
Brighton Business School, Mithras House, Lewes Road, Brighton, Sussex
BN2 4AT. Tel: 01273 642572

UNIVERSITY OF CENTRAL ENGLAND IN BIRMINGHAM
(full-time/part-time)
Franchise Street, Perry Barr, Birmingham B42 2SU. Tel: 0121 331 6646

UNIVERSITY OF CENTRAL LANCASHIRE (full-time and part-time)
Preston, PR1 2TQ. Tel: 01772 201201

CITY UNIVERSITY (full-time and part-time)
Northampton Square, London EC1V 0HB. Tel: 020 7040 8301

THE COLLEGE OF LAW
(full-time and distance learning)
(Branches at Store Street, London; Guildford; Chester; York and
Birmingham)
All enquiries should be addressed to the Registrar, Braboeuf Manor, St
Catherine's, Guildford, Surrey GU3 1HA. Tel: 01483 460200

DE MONTFORT UNIVERSITY (full-time/part-time/distance learning)
The Gateway, Leicester LE1 9BH. Tel: 0116 255 1551

UNIVERSITY OF EAST ANGLIA (full-time)
Norwich, NR4 7TJ. Tel: 01603 593042

UNIVERSITY OF EXETER (full-time)
Amory Building, Rennes Drive, Exeter EX4 4RJ. Tel: 01392 263263

UNIVERSITY OF GLAMORGAN (full-time/part-time)
Pontypridd, Mid Glamorgan CF37 1DL. Tel: 01443 480480

HOLBORN COLLEGE (part-time)
(franchised by University of Wolverhampton)
200 Greyhound Road, London W14 9RY. Tel: 020 7385 3377

UNIVERSITY OF HUDDERSFIELD (full-time/part-time/distance
learning)
Queensgate, Huddersfield HD1 3DH. Tel: 01484 422288

UNIVERSITY OF KEELE (full-time)
Keele, Staffordshire ST5 5BG
Tel: 01782 621111

KINGSTON UNIVERSITY (full-time and evening part-time)
Kingston upon Thames, Surrey KT2 7LB
Tel: 020 8547 2000

LEEDS METROPOLITAN UNIVERSITY (full-time/part-time)
School of Law, Leeds Metropolitan University, Beckett Park Campus,
Leeds LS6 3QS
Tel: 0113 283 2600

LONDON GUILDHALL UNIVERSITY (full time/part-time)
84 Moorgate, London EC2M 6SQ. Tel: 020 7320 1000

MANCHESTER METROPOLITAN UNIVERSITY (full-time/part-time/distance learning)
School of Law, Elizabeth Gaskell Campus, Hathersage Road,
Manchester M13 0JA
Tel: 0161 247 3049

MIDDLESEX UNIVERSITY (full-time)
Middlesex Business School, The Burroughs, London NW4 4BT. Tel: 020 8368 1299

UNIVERSITY OF NORTH LONDON (full-time/part-time)
School of Law, 62–66 Ladbrooke House, Highbury Grove, London N5 2AD
Tel: 020 7602 2789 Extn: 5103

UNIVERSITY OF NORTHUMBRIA AT NEWCASTLE (full-time/part-time/distance learning)
Ellison Building, Ellison Place, Newcastle upon Tyne NE1 8ST. Tel: 0191 232 6002

NOTTINGHAM TRENT UNIVERSITY (full-time/part-time/distance learning)
Burton Street, Nottingham NG1 4BU. Tel: 0115 941 8418

OXFORD BROOKES UNIVERSITY (full-time/part-time)
Gipsy Lane, Headington, Oxford OX3 0BP. Tel: 01865 741111

SOUTH BANK UNIVERSITY (full-time/part-time)
Borough Road, London SE1 0AA. Tel: 020 7928 8989

STAFFORDSHIRE UNIVERSITY (full-time/part-time)
Leek Road, Stoke on Trent ST4 2DF. Tel: 01782 294550

UNIVERSITY OF SUSSEX (full-time)
Arts Building, Falmer, Brighton BN1 9QN. Tel: 01273 606755

THAMES VALLEY UNIVERSITY (full-time/part-time)
St Mary's Road, Ealing, London WR5 5RF. Tel: 020 8579 5000

UNIVERSITY OF WEST OF ENGLAND (full-time/part-time/distance learning)
School of Law, Frenchay. Bristol BS16 1QY. Tel: 0117 965 6261

UNIVERSITY OF WESTMINSTER (full-time/part-time)
Regent Campus, Central Office, University of Westminster, 16 Riding House Street, London W19 7PT. Tel: 020 7911 5000 Extn: 2615

UNIVERSITY OF WOLVERHAMPTON (full-time/part-time)
Arthur Storer Building, Molineux Street, Wolverhampton MV1 1SB. Tel: 01902 321999

WORCESTER COLLEGE OF TECHNOLOGY (part-time)
(franchised by Staffordshire University)
Deansway, Worcester WR1 2JF. Tel: 01905 723383

INSTITUTIONS PROVIDING LPC COURSES

Anglia Polytechnic University
Enquiries
Marian Scott, The Course Administrator, Legal Practice Course, Anglia Law School, Anglia Polytechnic University, Bishops Hall Lane, Chelmsford, Essex CM1 1SQ
Tel: 01245 493 131 ext. 3206
Fax: 01245 493 134

Bournemouth University
Enquiries
Course Administrator, Department of Finance and Law, Dorset House,
Talbot Campus, Wallisdown, Poole, Dorset BH12 5BB
Tel: 01202 595 543/01202 595 187
Fax: 01202 595 261

BPP Law School
Enquiries
Ms Natasha Braithwaite, Full-time LPB Registrar, 67–69 Lincolns Inn
Fields, London EC1A 3JB
Tel: 020 7430 2304
Fax: 020 7404 1389

Cardiff University
Cardiff Law School
Enquiries
Mr Bryon Jones, Centre for Professional Legal Studies, Cardiff Law
School, PO Box 294, Cardiff CF10 3UX
Tel: 029 2087 4941
Fax: 029 2087 4984

University of Central England in Birmingham
Enquiries
Admissions Officer, Faculty of Law and Social Sciences, Dawson
Building, University of Central England, Perry Barr, Birmingham B42 2SU
Tel: 0121 331 6439
Fax: 0121 331 6438

The College of Law – Birmingham
Enquiries
Mrs Claire Hinwood, The Admission Department, The College of Law,
Braboeuf Manor, Portsmouth Road, Guildford, Surrey GU3 1HA
Tel: 0800 328 0153
Fax: 01483 460 460
E-mail: info@lawcol.co.uk

The College of Law – Chester
Enquiries
Mrs Claire Hinwood, The Admission Department, The College of Law,
Braboeuf Manor, Portsmouth Road, Guildford, Surrey GU3 1HA
Tel: 0800 328 0153
Fax: 01483 460 460
E-mail: info@lawcol.co.uk

The College of Law – Guildford
Enquiries
Mrs Claire Hinwood, The Admission Department, The College of Law,
Braboeuf Manor, Portsmouth Road, Guildford, Surrey GU3 1HA
Tel: 0800 328 0153
Fax: 01483 460 460
E-mail: info@lawcol.co.uk

The College of Law – London
Enquiries
Mrs Claire Hinwood, The Admission Department, The College of Law,
Braboeuf Manor, Portsmouth Road, Guildford, Surrey GU3 1HA
Tel: 0800 328 0153
Fax: 01483 460 460
E-mail: info@lawcol.co.uk

The College of Law – York
Enquiries
Mrs Claire Hinwood, The Admission Department, The College of Law,
Braboeuf Manor, Portsmouth Road, Guildford, Surrey GU3 1HA
Tel: 0800 328 0153
Fax: 01483 460 460
E-mail: info@lawcol.co.uk

De Montford University in association with the University of Birmingham
Enquiries
Rachel Bathers, University of Birmingham, Professional Legal Studies
Centre, Metallurgy Building, Edgbaston, Birmingham B15 2TT
Tel: 0121 414 6870
Fax: 0121 414 6871
E-mail: bathersr@lpc.bham.ac.uk

De Montford University in association with the University of Bristol
Enquiries
Maurice Cook/Karen Pope, Department of Professional Legal Studies,
c/o University of Bristol, University Gate, Park Row, Clifton, Bristol
BS1 5UB
Tel: 0117 954 5361
Fax: 0117 925 6717
E-mail: kpope@dmu.ac.uk and cmizen@dmu.ac.uk

De Montford University, Leicester
Enquiries
Jane Franks, Department of Professional Legal Studies, School of Law,
De Montford University, The Gateway, Leicester LE1 9BH
Tel: 0116 257 7177 ext. 8214
Fax: 0116 257 7186

University of Exeter
Enquiries
The Secretary, Centre for Legal Practice, Amory Building, Rennes Drive,
Exeter EX4 4RJ
Tel: 01392 263 157
Fax: 01392 263 196

University of Glamorgan
Enquiries
LPC Admissions Secretary, School of Law, University of Glamorgan,
Pontypridd, South Wales CF37 1DL
Tel: 01443 483 007
Fax: 01443 483 008

University of Hertfordshire
Enquiries
Mr Michael Hackett, Admissions Tutor, Faculty of Law, University of
Hertfordshire
Tel: 01707 286 215
Fax: 01707 286 205
E-mail: m.hackett@herts.ac.uk

University of Huddersfield
Enquiries
Mrs Vivienne Wild, Department of Law, The University of Huddersfield,
Queensgate, Huddersfield HD1 3DH
Tel: 01484 472 634/01484 472 192
Fax: 01484 472 279

Inns of Court School of Law
Enquiries
Admissions, Inns of Court Law School, 4 Gray's Inn Place, London
WC1R 5DX
Tel: 020 7404 5787
Fax: 020 7831 4188
E-mail: Lpc@icsl.ac.uk
Internet: www.icsl.ac.uk

University of Central Lancashire
Enquiries
Admissions Tutor (LPC), Department of Legal Studies, University of
Central Lancashire, Corporation Street, Preston PR1 2HE
Tel: 01772 893 060
Fax: 01772 892 908

Leeds Metropolitan University
Enquiries
Leeds Metropolitan University, Faculty of Business, School of Law,
Cavendish Hall, Beckett Park Campus, Otley Road, Leeds LS6 3QS
Tel: 0113 283 7549
Fax: 0113 283 3206

*Liverpool John Moores University based on Nottingham Law Schools
materials*
Enquiries
Miss Lynda Cunningham/Miss Mandy Smith, School of Law and
Applied Social Studies, Liverpool John Moores University, Josephine
Butler House, 1 Myrtle Street, Liverpool L7 4DN
Tel: 0151 231 3950/3923/3976
Fax: 0151 231 3908/3968

London Guildhall University
Enquiries
Legal Practice Course Administrator, London Guildhall University,
Department of Law, 84 Moorgate, London EC2M 6SQ
Tel: 020 7320 1544
Fax: 020 7320 1525

The Manchester Metropolitan University
Enquiries
LPC Admissions, The School of Law, The Manchester Metropolitan
University, Elizabeth Gaskell Campus, Hathersage Road, Manchester
M13 0JA
Tel: 0161 247 3047
Fax: 0161 247 6309

University of Northumbria at Newcastle
Enquiries
Ms Dawn Haynes, School of Law, Sutherland Building, University of
Northumbria, Newcastle upon Tyne NE1 8ST
Tel: 0191 227 3490
Fax: 0191 227 4557

Nottingham Law School
Nottingham Trent University
Enquiries
Nottingham Law School Ltd, Nottingham Trent University, Belgrave
Centre, Chaucer Street, Nottingham NG1 5LP
Tel: 0115 848 6871 ext. 4167
Fax: 0115 848 6878
Internet: www.nls.ntu.ac.uk

*Oxford Institute of Legal Practice (a joint foundation of the University of
Oxford and Oxford Brookes University)*
Enquiries
The Administrator, Oxford Institute of Legal Practice, King Charles
House, Park End Street, Oxford OX1 1JD
Tel: 01865 260 000
Fax: 01865 260 002

The University of Sheffield
Enquiries
Admissions Office, University of Sheffield, Faculty of Law,
Crookesmoor Building, Conduit Road, Sheffield S10 1FL
Tel: 0114 222 6770
Fax: 0114 222 6832

South Bank University/University of North London
Enquiries
LPC Course Administrator, South Bank University, Borough Road,
London SE1 0AA
Tel: 020 7815 8211
Fax: 020 7815 7793

Staffordshire University
Enquiries
LPC Admissions Section, Law School, Staffordshire University, Leek
Road, Stoke on Trent ST4 2DF
Tel: 01782 294 452
E-mail: r.s.evans@staffs.ac.uk

Thames Valley University
Enquiries
Mary Johnstone, Admissions Legal Practice Course, School of Law,
Thames Valley University, St Mary's Road, Ealing, London W5 5RF
Tel: 020 8231 2592
Fax: 020 8231 2553

University of the West of England, Bristol
Enquiries
Mr Luke Champion (Course Administrator), Faculty of Law, University
of the West of England, Frenchay Campus, Coldharbour Lane, Bristol
BS16 1QY
Tel: 0117 965 6261
Fax: 0117 976 3841

University of Westminster
Enquiries
Miles McLeod, LPC Resource Room, School of Law, University of
Westminster, 4 Little Titchfield Street, London W1W 7UW
Tel: 020 7911 5017
Fax: 020 7911 5175
E-mail: lpcadmin@wmin.ac.uk
Internet: http://www.wmin.ac.uk/law

University of Wolverhampton
Enquiries
Ms Kay Meredith, LPC Secretary, School of Legal Studies, University of
Wolverhampton, Molineux Street, Wolverhampton, West Midlands
WV1 1SB
Tel: 01902 321 503
Fax: 01902 322 696

HOW TO BECOME A BARRISTER

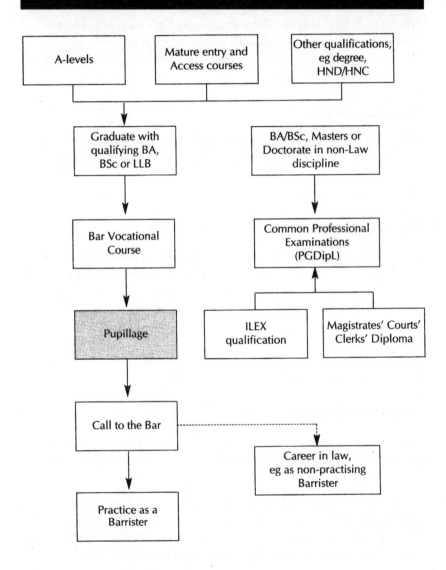

Main routes to qualifying as a barrister

MAIN ROUTES TO QUALIFYING AS A BARRISTER

A-levels and equivalents

Nearly all A-level subjects are acceptable. But it is most important to achieve excellent grades, preferably grades A and B to stand a good chance of getting into a well-respected university and course. See p.26 for a list of qualifying law degrees.

Access courses

Many universities encourage mature students to apply for entry. Some of these mature students will have attended an Access Course that has prepared them for higher education and further study. Previous relevant experience can sometimes put such applicants at an advantage.

The law degree

If you wish to qualify as a barrister you must be a graduate. Most, but not all, barristers will have studied a law degree (LLB). There are numerous varieties of law degrees, some concentrating on traditional law subjects, others include a variety of options. It is important to make sure that it is a Qualifying Law Degree. You can do this by checking with The General Council of the Bar. See Chapter 11 for the address. Try to aim for at least an upper second class degree as you will find it more difficult to obtain pupillage with a lower second or below.

The CPE/Diploma in Law

A significant number of barristers hold a degree in a subject other than law. Again it is very important to obtain a good class of degree, ideally an upper second or above.

Graduates who have not obtained a law degree need to take an extra qualification in law. This is either the Common Professional Examination (CPE) or the Diploma in Law. Both courses normally last one year full-time or two years part-time. See page 40 for a list of providers.

The Bar Vocational Course (BVC)

To become a barrister entitled to practise, the Bar Council requires you to take the one-year Bar Vocational Course (BVC). Before you start the BVC you will need to join one of the four Inns of Court – Lincoln's Inn, Inner Temple, Middle Temple or Gray's Inn (all based in London). These provide collegiate activities, support for barristers and student members, advocacy training and other continuing professional development opportunities. The Inns also provide the mechanism by which students become barristers, known as 'Call to the Bar', once they have completed the BVC and pupillage. The BVC aims to help you gain the skills of advocacy, conference skills, drafting, fact management, legal research, negotiation, and opinion writing to prepare you for the practical stage of training on the job, the one year of pupillage.

Pupillage

Pupillage is the final stage to qualifying as a barrister and is hard work. Pupillage involves observing a senior barrister (your 'pupil' master) at work for six months (unpaid). During the first six months you will be expected to undertake legal research, draft opinions, and read your pupil master's paperwork. Once you have satisfied the first six months, you will, with your pupil master's permission practice as a barrister and even appear in court as an advocate. This is when you start to build your own reputation and have your own cases.

Self-employed barristers usually group together to form a set of chambers, in which members will share office accommodation and overheads. Every chamber has an experienced barrister at its head. There will be a number of members of varying seniority with a number of clerks who are responsible for the administration work. Permanent members of a set of chambers are known as tenants and temporary members are known as squatters.

Those of you keen to become a barrister are in for a tough time. Competition for places is keen. In the 2005/2006 academic year there will be 1,594 places. The BVC is available at eight different teaching institutions throughout the country; see the list on page 57. Prior to 1998 the Inns of Court School of Law was the only provider. On completion of the BVC, a high proportion of people will be unable to get 'pupillage' but may be able to work for a legal department in a major company. Full details about each institution can be found at www.lawzone.co.uk/barcouncil.

In March 2001, the Bar Council introduced a new pupillage application system. All pupillage vacancies are now advertised on the OLPAS (Online Pupillage Application System) website – www.olpas.co.uk. *The Pupillage & Awards Handbook* acts as a companion to the OLPAS website. OLPAS allows you to submit online applications to up to to 12 sets of chambers in each recruitment season. Before applying find out as much as possible about your preferred set of chambers. You can access the chambers' website or online Bar Directory, or attend a Pupillage Fair. For dates and venues of Fairs see www.doctorjob.com/targetlive/pupillagefairs.

CASE STUDY

Bar Vocational Course student

Kim ran her own prosperous car spraying business for five years before deciding to embark on the long and uncertain route to the Bar. She successfully completed the BVC at the College of Law in 1998 and is now on her first six-month pupillage. Why was Kim so determined to become a barrister? 'One of the options in my Institute of the Motor Industry exams focused on law and I've been fascinated by it ever since. The experiences of a friend who is a barrister also inspired me – what also appealed was the variety of work you deal with, being self-employed and the challenges that the Bar presents.'

Kim gave up her business to undertake a law degree at Middlesex University as a mature student. She was keen to gain experience from different sets of chambers. 'I prepared early and spent a lot of time during the third year of university applying for mini pupillages – I did 14 before starting at The College of Law. It gave me the ideal opportunity to learn about different chambers, what kind of work they do and how they function.' Kim chose to study the BVC at the College the first year the course was offered. 'The course was opening up to new providers and I wanted to be part of the innovative teaching methods that were being offered by the College. I also chose The College of Law because of its reputation in the legal community.' The BVC was a challenge. The sheer volume of work and the fact that she was constantly learning new skills made it hard, but also rewarding. 'Overall I really enjoyed the course. It was hard work, especially learning new skills such as drafting and opinion writing. Everything had a practical approach which is different from most academic study. We also worked in small groups which was an excellent way to practise these new skills.'

FUNDING

Money is an extra hurdle. You'll need a fair amount of it to see you through since the fees alone for the BVC are in the region of £7,000 – £9,000. Those without a Qualifying Law Degree will have an extra year's training to pay for when studying for the CPE or Diploma in Law. The average cost of completing the vocational stage of training is estimated at over £18,000 if living expenses are taken into account. Only a limited number of awards, grants and scholarships are available for the vocational stage of Bar training. See the section on funding in the previous chapter (page 23). In addition refer to the *Chambers Pupillage and Awards Handbook* and to the Bar Council Scholarship Trust – further details from the Bar Council.

CASE STUDY

Barrister

Claire is a barrister at Blackstone Chambers specialising in employment law. She was called to the bar in 1998 and secured a tenancy with Blackstone that same year.

She chose A-levels in French, Russian and Latin and obtained three A grades. Claire chose a BA in Law (European Option) at Queen's College, Cambridge, spending her third year at the University of Poitiers, France. She got an upper second in her first year and a first in her final year. She later did a Masters in Law at Harvard, doing a mixture of antitrust and constitutional law/civil liberties.

Before going to Harvard Claire took a year off. 'After I left college I wasn't sure I wanted to practise law, so I spent a year working for Lord Lester of Herne Hill QC, doing political research and writing speeches on various topics such as human rights and discrimination. I then decided that the Bar probably was for me, so I went to Bar School.'

'In the summers after my second and third years at college I spent time at Simmons & Simmons in Paris, Baker & McKenzie in London, Freshfields in London, and Coudert Brothers in London, because at that stage I thought I wanted to use my languages and possibly work in an overseas office. I then decided to go to the Bar instead, and spent time before my fourth year at Monckton Chambers and Brick Court Chambers. During Bar School I did mini-pupillages at 2 Temple Gardens, Monckton Chambers, Brick Court Chambers, Essex Court Chambers and Blackstone Chambers.' Claire found her summer experience to be invaluable not only in giving her CV further credibility but also in helping her decide whether to be a solicitor or barrister. 'I initially thought I wanted to use my languages, and being a solicitor was the only realistic option if I wanted to live abroad and still practise law. Having done a number of summer placements, however, I realised that I was perhaps not ideally suited to working in a corporate environment. I also wanted the chance, having formulated the arguments in a case, to be able to put them to a judge, and was concerned that if I did not at least try to become a barrister I might always have wondered what it would have been like. Finally, having decided, more or less on the eve of having to fill in the application forms for solicitors' firms, that I wanted to try the Bar instead, I spoke to my Dad who suggested that the Bar was too uncertain and a bad career for a woman – there was no better way of ensuring that his extremely stubborn daughter would choose the Bar.'

'When I was at Bar School there was only one option, namely the ICSL. I spent a lot of my time that year doing part-time research jobs to cover the cost of the year over and above the scholarship which my Inn had generously given me, so I probably didn't give the ICSL a fair chance. In general, however, it was not a particularly interesting year.'

Claire's interest in human rights began at College, and her work experience with Lord Lester dealing with public law assisted her decision to focus on public law and employment law.'I knew a little bit about Blackstone Chambers from my work with Lord Lester, and at the time I was applying for pupillage there were few chambers which were as good as Blackstone concentrating on commercial, employment and public law. Finally, when I came for a mini-pupillage I liked the atmosphere, particularly amongst the junior tenants. You need to enjoy spending time with your colleagues in every profession, but in view of the size of most chambers, and the slow rate of turnover, you have to be really sure that these are people you would enjoy going for a drink with.'

A typical day or week for Claire varies greatly depending on whether she is in court or in a tribunal – last week involved a conference with a QC about disclosure of the electoral roll and the ECHR; drafting an originating application to an employment tribunal in an unfair dismissal case; drafting grounds of resistance for a company on the other side of a similar case; settling a long-standing disability discrimination case for an applicant shortly before the hearing; preparing a judicial review for the Legal Services Commission; and preparing a possible injunction with a QC to enforce restrictive covenants against an ex-employee. It also involved various bits and pieces of advisory work, including advising on witness statements for a forthcoming seven-day disability discrimination hearing. Her hours are irregular and she frequently works in the evenings and at the weekend.

QUALIFYING AS AN ADVOCATE IN SCOTLAND

The intending advocate in Scotland needs to take an LLB degree followed by the postgraduate Diploma in Legal Practice plus one or two years training in Scotland in a solicitor's office. It is advised that intending advocates practise as solicitors for a period before going to the Bar. This is followed by further unpaid practical training called 'devilling' to an experienced advocate in combination with sitting the Faculty of Advocates' written examinations. Contact the Faculty of Advocates for further information. See 'Finding out More...' for the address.

QUALIFYING AS A BARRISTER IN NORTHERN IRELAND

The Institute of Professional Legal Studies at the Queen's University of Belfast offers a one-year postgraduate course of vocational training for both trainee barristers and trainee solicitors. Anyone who intends to enter either branch of the legal profession in Northern Ireland must attend the Institute and successfully complete the course that leads to the award of the Certificate in Professional Legal Studies which is a one-year course. Bar trainees spend a week work-shadowing a practising barrister immediately prior to commencing their course. A further period of in-practice training starts after graduation from the Institute and takes the form of a 12-month pupillage.

All applicants must hold a recognised law degree or hold a degree in any subject other than law and have successfully completed a course of legal study approved by the Council of Legal Education (Northern Ireland). For further information contact the Institute of Professional Legal Studies. See 'Finding out More...' for the address.

INSTITUTIONS OFFERING THE BAR VOCATIONAL COURSE

BPP Law School
68–70 Red Lion Street, London WC1R 4NY
Tel: 020 7430 2304
Fax: 020 7404 1389
Course Leader: Richard Holt
Places: 216
Admin Contact: Louise Wodehouse-Easton (e-mail louisewe@bpp.com)

Cardiff Law School
Centre for Professional Legal Studies, Cardiff Law School, PO Box 294,
Cardiff CF1 3UX
Tel: 029 2087 4964
Fax: 029 2087 4984

The College of Law
50–52 Chancery Lane, London WC2A 1SX
Tel: 020 7969 3100
Freephone: 0800 289 997
Course Leader: Sarah Macdonald
Places: 120
Admin Contact: Sue Drury (e-mail: susan.drury@lawcol.co.uk)
From August 2002 courses will be held at: 14 Store Street, London
WC1E 7DE

Inns of Court School of Law
4 Gray's Inn Place, London WC1R 5DX
Tel: 020 7404 5787
Fax: 020 7831 4188
Course Leader: Rosie Smawell-Smith
Places: 575 full time; 75 part-time (2 year course)
Admin Contact: Victoria Goodyear (e-mail v.goodyear@icsl.ac.uk)

Manchester Metropolitan University
Elizabeth Gaskell Campus, Hathersage Road, Manchester M12 0JA
Tel: 0161 247 3053
Fax: 0161 247 6879
Course Leader: Alan Gibb
Places: 100
Admin Contact: Lucy Holland (e-mail: l.holland@mmu.ac.uk)

University of Northumbria
School of Law, Sutherland Building, Northumberland Road, Newcastle
upon Tyne NE1 8ST
Tel: 0191 227 3939
Fax: 0191 227 4557

Course Leader: Andrea O'Caine
Places: 80 + 20 exempting
Admin Contact: Margaret Bell (e-mail: margaret.bell@unn.ac.uk)

Nottingham Law School
Belgrave Centre, Chaucer Street, Nottingham NG1 5LP
Tel: 0115 848 6871
Fax: 0115 848 6878
Course Leader: Tessa Williamson
Places: 120
Admin Contact: Hazel Vedmore (e-mail: hazel.vedmore@ntu.ac.uk)

University of the West of England, Bristol
Faculty of Law, Frenchay Campus, Coldharbour Lane, BS16 1QT
Tel: 0117 965 6261 x 3769
Fax: 0117 344 2268
Course Leader: Stephen Migdal
Places: 96
Admin Contact: Gabriel Fallon (e-mail: gabriel.fallon@uwe.ac.uk)
Course Leader: Angela Devereux
Places: 60
Admin Contact: Zoe Selley (e-mail: selly@cardiff.ac.uk)

GETTING WORK EXPERIENCE

Getting work experience is crucial in terms of helping you secure a training contract or pupillage in today's extremely competitive climate. It is not enough to be purely a brilliant academic. The more relevant experience you have, the better the chance of succeeding.

What have you got to gain from work experience?

- It will give you a real insight into the profession and whether or not that is what you want to do. Some real experience will be particularly useful if you are trying to weigh up the pros and cons of qualifying as a barrister or solicitor.

- It helps you to make a better transition into your eventual move into the world of full-time work.

- It gives you the opportunity to build up those all-important contacts.

- It will help you to gain excellent (hopefully!) references.

However, it is not that easy getting legal work experience. Most employers recognise this and do not stipulate that it is essential although it is preferred. But if you can't get experience in a firm of solicitors or chambers, any work experience that demonstrates use of the skills they are interested in will be valuable. Skills such as communications skills, determination, business awareness, IT skills can all be developed in many other sectors of business and commerce.

You can also gain relevant experience and knowledge at university and/or BVC by participating in debating, mooting, Inn advocacy weekends, mock trials and reading the legal pages in newspapers regularly.

WHERE TO APPLY FOR WORK EXPERIENCE

- Placement in a firm of solicitors
- Mini-pupillage in chambers
- Paralegals and Outdoor Clerks
- Barrister's Clerk
- The Law Commission
- Law Centres
- Citizens Advice Bureaux
- Voluntary work in charitable organisations.

MARKETING YOURSELF

There is no one guaranteed way of succeeding in getting work experience so try as many as you can think of and be creative in the process. Here are a few suggestions:

- Ask your teachers at school/college if they have any contacts in the legal profession.
- Use your Careers Service and speak to your careers officer.
- Talk to your family and friends and ask them if they can suggest anyone to contact.
- Make sure everyone you know is aware you are looking for work experience.
- Send your CV to firms of solicitors. *Chambers and Partners Directory* will give you names and addresses of solicitors firms.
- Send your CV to chambers. *Chambers and Partners Directory* will give you names and addresses of chambers.
- Keep up-to-date with the profession by reading the 'quality press' on their relevant legal days and look at specialist journals such as *The Law Society Gazette* and *The Lawyer* which should both be available from large public libraries.

Perhaps you could ask to go in for one or two weeks' work experience during the holidays or even ask for one day's work shadowing to get an insight into what the working environment is like. Whichever route you take will almost certainly be on a voluntary basis unless you have specific skills to offer, such as good office and keyboard skills, in which case you could try to get some paid work with a firm of solicitors during the summer or register with an employment agency.

HOW TO APPLY

It's never too early to start to put together a curriculum vitae (CV). This is a summary of what you have done in your life to date, so if you have hardly any work experience then one page on good quality A4 paper will be sufficient. If you are a mature student with a lot of jobs behind you there is sometimes a case for going onto a second page, but for most of you a one page CV will be appropriate. So what should go into your CV? Here are the main headings:

Name
Address and telephone number
Date of birth
Nationality
Education and qualifications

Start with your present course of study and work back to the beginning of secondary school. No primary schools please! List the qualifications with grades you already have and the ones you intend to sit.

Work experience

Start with the most recent. Don't worry if you've only had a Saturday job at the local shop or a paper round. Put it all down. Employers would rather see that you've done something.

Skills

List those such as computer skills, software packages used, languages, driving licence.

Interests and positions of responsibility

What do you like to do in your spare time? If you are or have been captain of a sports team, been a committee member or even Head Boy or Girl at school, put it all down.

Referees

Usually two: an academic referee such as a teacher or head of your school plus someone who knows you well personally, who is not a relative, such as someone you have worked for.

Always highlight your good points on a CV and don't leave gaps. Always account for your time. If something such as illness prevented you from reaching your potential in your exams, point this out in the covering letter (see below). Lawyers have excellent attention to detail so make sure your spelling and grammar are perfect!

THE COVERING LETTER

Every CV or application form should always be accompanied by a covering letter. The letter is important because it is usually the first thing a potential employer reads. Here are some tips:

- The letter should be on the same A4 plain paper as your CV and should look like a professional document. No lined paper please! One side A4 only.
- Try to find out the name of the person you should send your letter and CV to. It makes a great difference to the reader the more you can personalise your application. If you start the letter 'Dear Mr Brown' remember you should finish it 'Yours sincerely'.
- First paragraph should tell the reader why you are contacting them
- Second paragraph should give them some information to make them interested in you such as highlight your interest in law along with some specific IT skills.
- Say in the letter if you already know anything about the firm or have read anything in the press recently that was relevant.
- Employers accept typed letters, unless they specifically request one to be handwritten.

A SAMPLE CV

There is no standard CV but here is a sample:

PERSONAL DETAILS

Name	Simon Anthony TATE
Address	134 Hillhouse Avenue Portsmouth POI 2TQ
Telephone No	01245 879476
Date of Birth	10 June 1981
Nationality	British

EDUCATION & QUALIFICATIONS

1993–1999	Linfield High School, Portsmouth
1999	A-levels English, History, French Eight GCSEs English (A), Mathematics (B), History (A), Geography (C), Chemistry (B), Biology (B), French (A), Latin (A)

WORK EXPERIENCE

1995 & 1996	Delivering newspapers and magazines throughout my local area
1997 & 1998	(Saturdays) Sales assistant in busy dry cleaners in centre of Portsmouth
August 1998	Two weeks as a temporary receptionist in a small firm of accountants, responsible for answering telephone and general clerical work

SKILLS — Languages – good written and spoken French
Computing – competent in MS Word and Excel

POSITIONS OF RESPONSIBILITY
Captain of football team at school

INTERESTS — Football, swimming, reading, particularly Jane Austen, and travelling to other countries such as America and France

REFERENCES — Available on request

CHOOSING YOUR UNIVERSITY LAW COURSE

In the late 1980s, demand for trainee solicitors briefly exceeded supply. Virtually anyone could pick up a training contract (then called 'articles') if they had the necessary qualifications. These days, however, competition is tough, and you'll need to show lots of ability and drive to impress your potential employers. The situation for budding barristers is similar.

But there is a positive side:

- Employers are generally impressed by a good calibre law graduate since law is known to be a challenging discipline requiring skills such as research, analysis, application, clarity, advocacy and effective written communication. These are very relevant in other jobs, so on the one hand you don't need a law degree to enter the profession, but on the other, law can be your springboard into a wide range of career possibilities.
- Some parts of the legal profession are growing, with law firms becoming more international and opening offices overseas (particularly in Eastern Europe) and expanding in areas such as Environmental Law and Intellectual Property Law.

The road to qualifying as a barrister or solicitor may not be easy, but the professional rewards can be great. If you are undeterred and still have your heart set on a law degree in some shape or form then it's time to start thinking about your next steps.

WHAT TO CONSIDER

The basic criteria for choosing your degree course are:

1. the kind of law course you are after
2. where you want to study
3. your academic ability.

Going to university is an investment, so it is worth giving these points some careful thought. But from the growing number of institutions offering law courses you will need to look at ways of narrowing down your options.

Once you have eliminated the bulk of the institutions and courses on offer start to carry out your own research:

- Contact your chosen universities or colleges and ask for their prospectuses (both official and alternative) and departmental brochures (if they exist) for more details. Remember that such publications are promotional and may be selective about the information they provide.
- Attend university open days if you can, and talk to former or current students. Try to imagine if you would be happy living for three years in that environment and address issues such as: Is it a campus or in a city? Will it allow you to pursue your interests?
- Talk to any legal practitioners you know and ask for their views on the reputations of different universities and courses.
- Visit the websites of the universities you are considering.
- Find out what academic criteria they are looking for and be realistic about the grades you are expecting. Your teachers at school or college will be able to advise you on this.

Once you have done this you should be able to produce a shortlist of universities and from that you can choose the top six places to put down on the UCAS form.

SUGGESTED TIMESCALE

Year 12

May/June: Do some serious thinking. Get ideas from friends, relatives, teachers, books etc. If possible visit some campuses before you go travelling!

June/July/ Make a shortlist of your courses.

August: Lay your hands on copies of the official and alternative (student-written) prospectuses and departmental brochures for extra details. They can usually be found in libraries but it's better to get your own sent to you. Look at the university department website.

Year 13

September:	Fill in your application form and send it off to UCAS – it will be accepted from 1 September onwards.
15 October:	Deadline for applying for places at Oxford or Cambridge.
15 January:	Deadline for submitting your applications to UCAS. They will consider late applications, but your chances are limited since some of the places will have already gone.
November:	Universities hold their open days and sometimes interviews.
April:	Decisions will begin to go directly to the candidates.
By 15 May:	Or within two weeks of the final decision you receive, you must tell UCAS (assuming you've had some offers) which offer you have accepted firmly and which one is your back-up.
Spring:	Fill in yet more forms – this time the grant forms which you can get from your school, college or LEA.
Summer:	Sit your exams and wait for the results. UCAS will get in touch by early September and tell you whether your chosen universities or colleges have confirmed your conditional offers. Don't be too disappointed if you haven't got in. Just get in touch with your school, college or careers office and wait until clearing starts in September when any left-over places are filled. You will be sent instructions on clearing automatically, but it's up to you to get hold of the published list of unfilled places and contact the universities directly.

For more details about UCAS and filling in your applications see *How to Complete Your UCAS Form* by Tony Higgins (see Useful Books at the back of this book).

DIFFERENT KINDS OF LAW COURSES AVAILABLE

a) Course content – Single or Joint Honours?

All the institutions listed in this guide on page 26 offer Qualifying Law Degrees as recognised by the Law Society and the Bar Council. This means that you can select the required courses that will exempt you from taking the Common Professional Examination (CPE) after you graduate. The seven foundations of legal knowledge are Contract, Tort (often both are referred to as Obligations), Criminal Law, Constitutional & Administrative Law (or Public Law), Property Law (or Land Law), Equity & Trusts, and Law of the European Union.

Law can be taken on its own or mixed with a number of other subjects. It can be difficult to decide whether to study law by itself (a Single Honours degree), with another subject (Joint or Combined degree) or as part of a modular programme, alongside a multitude of topics.

If you are considering a Single Honours course, a good range of optional subjects might make it even more inviting. You don't want to be stuck with just a handful of choices from which to fill in your timetable after you've put down the core courses. And options may be law-related or from a completely different discipline. Some places can only offer a limited selection, while others provide a variety of law courses as well as the opportunities to take non-law courses.

Alternatively, if you want to specialise in one other area, then a Joint degree might be more appealing. Some Joint degrees do not require previous knowledge of the second subject. Others, especially those with a European language, often specify that candidates must have an A-level or GCSE for background knowledge. With Joint degrees, be wary of courses that have seemingly identical titles, for example, Law with German, Law and German, and Law and German Law. In the first one, law is the major subject; in the second, you'll probably spend equal time on each and in the third the stress is on law rather than German language. Any of them may involve some time abroad.

b) Black Letter, contextual and vocational approaches

It is worth knowing that there are broadly three different approaches to teaching law. But you cannot base your selection on this criterion since few institutions adhere to one kind. Most places are likely to opt for a mixture (sometimes even within an individual unit, especially if it is taught by several different tutors). It can be useful though to find out (perhaps during an open day) which attitude is prevalent. The categories are:

(i) Black Letter Law
This focuses on the core subjects and doesn't look much beyond statutes and legal reports for its sources of law. It may sound dry, but it should provide a thorough grounding in the English legal system.

(ii) Contextual approach
Some courses examine law in context, that's to say, law, its role and its effectiveness are looked at in relation to society (past and present), politics and the economy. Such courses may include elements of Critical Legal Theory. Students are expected to analyse the problems (for example, loopholes, contradictions, injustices and so on) within the law. This can make for some heated and controversial seminars.

(iii) Vocational approach
This stresses professional training and skills. It includes sandwich degrees with work placements and other degrees with units dedicated to lawyers' skills like negotiating, interviewing, counselling, drafting, research, analysis, clear expression, and the ability to read through vast amounts of material, sift out the legally relevant points and present a logical argument. Ironically, you will be able to pick up most of these skills through other standard law units and extra-curricular activities like mooting (a mock court room trial), debating and Law Clinics, in which students get the opportunity to help out with a real life case from start to finish.

c) Studying overseas and working placements

Studying overseas and/or completing a work placement could also be factors affecting your degree selection. Not all of these courses will send you off for a full year though. Neither must you be a linguist, since you can study or work overseas in English in, for example, North America, the Netherlands or Malaysia. The availability of student exchanges has increased through programmes such as Erasmus, which encourage universities to provide international opportunities where practicable. There are relatively few law degree courses which insist on work placements; however, some hands-on experience during holidays will prove invaluable and you should try to organise this yourself even if it is not a requirement of the course you choose. See the previous chapter.

WHERE YOU WANT TO STUDY

a) Which country and legal system?

If you're hoping to practise law then ask yourself where you intend to work – England or Wales? Northern Ireland? Scotland? Since the legal systems differ over Britain, it seems pointless to study in Aberdeen if you want to practise in Aberystwyth. Although, if you do need to move, then it is usually possible to transfer the legal skills and knowledge you already have and adapt them to the new place.

(i) England and Wales
See the chapters on how to become a solicitor and how to become a barrister.

(ii) Northern Ireland
Law in N. Ireland is very similar to that in England and Wales, but if you study in Ireland and want to practise over the water then you are obliged to sit an additional exam in Land Law. In 1977, the Institute of Professional Legal Studies was set up at Queen's University in Belfast by the Council of Legal Education. The Council runs a course that provides training for law graduates wishing to become legal practitioners. This vocational course leads to a Certificate in Professional Legal Studies. The core subjects you need to start the course are the same as in England plus Company Law (or Law of Business Organisations) and Law of Evidence. But if you haven't already done these then you have to take a preliminary course for a Certificate in Academic Legal Studies. After these certificates

you need to find a two-year apprenticeship to get your Restricted Practising Certificate so you can work as an assistant solicitor for a few years before eventually becoming a fully qualified solicitor.

(iii) Scotland

Being a lawyer in Scotland (solicitor or advocate) initially involves passing a number of core subjects. The Faculty of Advocates and the Law Society specify 11 common subjects plus two more each. After taking these within your degree there comes a one-year postgraduate practical course: a Diploma in Legal Practice. Beyond this, budding solicitors need a two-year traineeship to be fully qualified and advocates are required to do additional practical training and exams.

b) Various influencing factors

Once you've decided which country you'll be in, you can think about choosing specific institutions. But remember university life isn't going to be solely about academic study. It is truly a growing experience – educationally, socially, culturally – and besides, three or four years can really drag if you're not happy outside the lecture theatre. Below is an assortment of factors which might have some bearing on where you'd like to study. See which ones you think are relevant to you and try to put them in order of importance.

Educational facilities

Is there a well-stocked and up-to-date law library nearby or will you have to fight other law students for the materials? Check for access to computer terminals which you can use for improving the presentation of your dissertations, and availability of legal databases (such as Justis and Lexis). More vocational courses might also use mock court rooms with video and audio equipment. The facilities available will depend on the budget of an institution and plentiful resources tend to attract better tutors.

Quality of teaching

Difficult to establish without the benefit of an open day but the University Funding Council, an independent body set up by the government, has done the groundwork for you and assessed the level of teaching across the UK already. Their findings are publicly available from the External Relations Department, Higher Education Funding Council, Northaven House, Coldharbour Lane, Bristol BS16 1QD. Teaching quality may suffer if seminar or tutorial groups are too large, so try to compare group sizes for the same courses at different institutions.

Type of institution
There are basically three types.

- **'old' universities**
  Traditionally the more academic universities with higher admission requirements, the old universities are well established with good libraries and research facilities. They have a reputation for being resilient to change, but most are introducing modern elements into their degrees such as modular courses, an academic year split into two semesters, and programmes like Erasmus.

- **'new' universities**
  Pre-1992 these were polytechnics or institutes. They form a separate group because they still hold true to the original polytechnic doctrine of vocational courses and strong ties with industry, typically through placements and work experience. They are still looked down upon by some employers because of their generally lower academic entry requirements, but the new universities have a good name for flexible admissions and learning, modern approaches to their degrees and good pastoral care. Some law courses at these 'new' universities have been categorised as 'excellent' by the University Funding Council.

- **colleges of higher education**
  Usually these are specialist institutions and therefore provide excellent facilities in their chosen fields despite their size. They are sometimes affiliated to universities such as Holborn College and the University of Wolverhampton. This form of franchising means the college buys the right to teach the degree, which the university will award, provided that the course meets the standards set by the university.

Attractiveness to employers
Few employers will openly admit to giving preference to graduates from particular universities. Most are looking for high-quality degrees as an

indication of strong academic ability. But since students with higher A-level grades have tended to go to the old universities, it is unsurprising that a large proportion of successful lawyers come from traditional university backgrounds.

Full-time versus part-time and distance learning

Although most students prefer to study full time and finish their degrees in the shortest time possible, some people, for a variety of reasons, find it more convenient to study part time or from home or via the Internet. Only a limited number of institutions offer these options and they are listed in the earlier reference table.

Guaranteed place on LPC

Many universities have an arrangement with the College of Law which assures a place on an LPC to every student with a 2:2 degree or better. This is a good safety net to have if you fail to get a 2:1, but if you think you will have a problem getting a good law degree before you even start, then ask yourself if you wouldn't be happier and more successful studying another subject.

Non-academic considerations

■ **Finances**
   The cost of living isn't the same throughout the UK so will you be able to reach deeper into your pockets for rent or other fundamentals and entertainment if you are living in a major city or in the South?

■ **Friends and family**
   Do you want to get away from them or stay as close as possible? While there can be advantages, financial at least, to living at home, you may prefer the challenge of looking after yourself and the opportunity to be completely independent.

■ **Accommodation**
   Do you want to live on campus or in halls of residence with other students, or in private housing that you may need to organise yourself that could be a considerable distance from college? If your university is nearby, is there any point in moving away from home?

- **Entertainment**

  Are you going to be spending much time in, for example, the sports centre, the theatre or student bars? How about university societies – is there one that allows you to indulge your existing hobbies or the ones you've always dreamt of trying?

- **Site and size**

  Not usually a problem since many universities overcome the problems of urban v. rural and small v. large by locating their campus on the edge of a major town (e.g. University of Nottingham and University of Kent), and centralising certain facilities and services to ensure safety, convenience and some sense of community even on the largest and most widespread campus.

ACADEMIC ABILITY

For the majority of students, their A-level scores will be the deciding criteria for selection. And it's important to be realistic about the grades you're heading for: don't be too pessimistic, but don't kid yourself about your 'as yet undiscovered' genius. Talk to your teachers for an accurate picture of your predicted results.

Not one institution requires law A-level from potential students. Oddly, those of you with a little legal knowledge might even find yourselves at a disadvantage. Few courses specify subjects they want you to have studied (with the exception of most language Joint degrees), although traditional qualifications are welcomed everywhere. Conversely, some universities won't accept A-levels like general studies, or the less academic ones such as art.

If your A-level results effectively prevent you from taking a law degree, then it's time for a rethink. If you wanted to take a law degree with a view to entering the profession, then you could opt for the entry route with a non-law degree instead. Most employers stress that a large number of trainee solicitors and pupil barristers have a non-law degree. Even though the route might be longer and therefore more expensive (if sponsorship cannot be found), a graduate with, say, an upper second class Honours degree in philosophy is infinitely more likely to make a successful lawyer than someone who scraped a pass in their LLB. It is important to remember that since degree courses can change format frequently, you must check with universities directly to confirm their specific requirements.

Remember that if you intend to read a subject other than law, you will have to complete, following graduation in that discipline, a one-year postgraduate conversion course in law (CPE/Postgraduate Diploma in Law) before going on to a Legal Practice Course or Bar Vocational Course.

COMPLETING YOUR UCAS FORM

General advice on filling in your UCAS form is given in another guide in this series, *How to Complete Your UCAS Form*, by Tony Higgins, Chief Executive of UCAS (see Useful Books).

The following advice should help you complete Section 10 – your personal statement. This is your opportunity to explain to the university admissions staff why you want to study law.

The personal section of the UCAS form is the only chance you get to recommend yourself as a serious candidate worthy of a place, or at least, worthy of an interview. It is therefore vital that you think very carefully indeed about how to complete it so that it shows you in the best possible light. You must sell yourself to the department of law and make it hard for them not to take you.

For 2001 entry there were 16,452 applicants for a law degree. Yet only 14,137 of those applicants were successful in being offered a place. So you can understand how competitive applying for law is. Of those that were successful, nearly 3,000 applicants gained places through Clearing, and a high proportion of these would not have been placed at their first choice universities.

Obviously, there are as many ways of completing Section 10 as there are candidates. There are no rules as such, but there are recommendations that can be made. Universities are academic institutions and thus you must present yourself as a strong academic bet. The admissions tutor reading your form will want to know all the relevant information about you and will want some answers to the following questions:

- What is the strength of your commitment to academic study?
- Why do you wish to study law? Money, status, family traditions, the sound of your own voice and legal paraphernalia are not good reasons.
- What precisely is it about the law that interests you? Give details and examples referring to recent cases, controversies and debates.

76

- What do you hope to get out of three years of legal academic study?
- What legal cases have you followed in detail?
- What related material have you recently read and why did you appreciate it?
- What recent judgements have you admired recently and why?
- What legal controversies have excited you?
- Which particular branch of the law interests you most and – again – why?
- Which lawyers, either living or dead, have inspired you and for what reason?

Work experience is very useful as it demonstrates a commitment to the subject outside the classroom. Remember to include any experience, paid or voluntary. Explain concisely what your job entailed and what you got out of the whole experience. Even if you've not been able to get work experience, if you have spoken to anyone in the legal profession about their job then it is worth mentioning as it all builds up a picture of someone who is keen and has done some research. Wanting to be Ally McBeal or Rumpole is not a good enough reasons to convince a hardened admissions tutor of your commitment to a law degree!

Future plans, if any, should also be included on your form. Be precise. Again this will demonstrate a breadth of interest in the subject. For example: 'I am particularly interested in pursuing a career at the Bar. My enthusiasm was initially sparked off by my active participation in the Debating Society at school, of which I am President. I also follow the major legal cases in the newspapers and have visited the Old Bailey on a number of occasions.'

At least half of your section 10 should deal with material directly related to your chosen course. But the rest of the page should tell the admissions tutor all about what makes you who you are:

- What travel have you undertaken?
- What do you read?
- What sporting achievements do you have?
- What music do you like or play?

In all these areas give details.

'Last year I went to Paris and visited all the Impressionist galleries there. I relax by reading American short stories – Andre Dubus and Raymond Carver amongst others. My musical taste is largely focused on opera (I have seen 14 productions of 'The Magic Flute') and I would like to continue playing the cello in an orchestra at university. I would also enjoy the chance to play in a football team to keep myself fit.'

This is much more impressive than saying:

'Last year I went to France. I like reading and listening to music and sometimes I play football at weekends.'

GENERAL TIPS

- Take a photocopy of your personal statement so you can remind yourself of all the wonderful things you said about yourself, should you be called for interview!
- Do not add any additional pages.
- Make sure it's legible as the form will be reduced to half its original size before being passed to institutions.
- If you are planning to do so, state your reasons for applying for deferred entry and your plans for the year before entry. For example, you might be hoping to find some relevant work experience in a firm of solicitors followed by some time spent in Germany to brush up your conversational German language skills.
- If your school or college offers it, use the Electronic Application System (EAS). Further details are given in *How to Complete Your UCAS Form*.

SUCCEEDING AT INTERVIEW

THE ACADEMIC INTERVIEW

Outside Oxford and Cambridge, formal interviews are rarely part of the admissions process. Even at highly respected institutions such as King's College London and University College London, interviews are not the norm for all candidates and are usually reserved for those from a non-traditional background and some mature candidates. They are expensive and time-consuming for both the university and the applicants. However, although academic interviews are rare, they do occur, so if you're invited to attend for interview, here are some points to bear in mind.

- Remember that if you shine in your interview and impress the admissions staff, they may drop their grades slightly and make you a lower offer.
- Interviews need not be as daunting as you fear. Interviews are designed to help those asking the questions to find out as much about you as they can. It is important to have good eye-contact and confident body language and view it as a chance to put yourself across well rather than as an obstacle course designed to catch you out.
- Interviewers are more interested in what you know than what you do not. If you are asked a question you don't know the answer to, say so. To waffle simply wastes time and lets you down. To lie, of course, is even worse, especially for aspiring lawyers!
- Remember your future tutor might be amongst the people interviewing you. Enthusiasm and a strong commitment to your subject and, above all, a willingness to learn are extremely important attitudes to convey.
- An ability to think on your feet is vital ... another prerequisite for a good lawyer. Pre-learned answers never work. Putting forward an answer, using examples and factual knowledge to reinforce your points will impress interviewers far more. It is also sensible to admit defeat if your argument is demolished.

- It is possible to steer the interview yourself to some extent. If you are asked something you know nothing about, confidently replacing that question with another related one yourself shows enthusiasm.
- Essential preparation includes revision of the personal section of your UCAS form so don't include anything on your form you're unprepared to speak about at interview.
- Questions may well be asked on your extra-curricular activities. Most often, this is a tactic designed to put you at your ease and therefore your answers should be thorough and enthusiastic.
- At the end of the interview, you'll probably be asked if there is anything you would like to ask your interviewer. If there is nothing, then say that your interview has covered all that you had thought of. It is sensible though, to have one or two questions of a serious kind – to do with the course, the tuition and so on – up your sleeve. It is not wise, obviously, to ask them anything that you could and should have found out from the prospectus.
- Above all, end on a positive note and remember to smile!

PREPARATION FOR A LAW INTERVIEW

We are assuming that you will be taking a Single Honours Law degree, but if you have chosen a Joint or Combined Honours course obviously you will have to prepare yourself for questions on those subjects as well.

The interview is a chance for you to demonstrate knowledge of, commitment to and enthusiasm for the law. The only way to do this is to be extremely well-informed. Interviewers will want to know your reasons for wishing to study law and, possibly above all, they will be looking to see whether you have a mind capable of developing logical arguments and the ability to articulate such arguments powerfully and coherently.

Much of the practice of law in this country rests on an adversarial system so don't be surprised if you receive an adversarial interview. Remember to keep calm and think clearly!

Reasons for wishing to study law vary. A passion for courtroom drama, 'The Bill' or 'Kavanagh QC' is not enough. You need to think about the everyday practice of the law in this country and it is extremely useful to spend time talking with lawyers of all kinds and learning from them what is involved.

It is important to be aware of the many types of law that lawyers practice – criminal, contract, family, taxation… and be clear about the differences between them. The essential differences between barristers and solicitors must also be clear in your mind.

Use of the media

As a serious A-level candidate you should already be reading a 'quality' daily newspaper. *The Independent*, *The Times* and *The Guardian* all have law sections during the week. If you are really keen read the *Law Society Gazette* or *The Lawyer* which are published weekly. Following detailed law reports in the press will give you further insight into the ways in which the law is practised.

Regular listening to the radio and watching television are vital. Much of the news has legal implications and these subjects are consistently discussed in the broadcast media. TV's 'Question Time', 'Newsnight' and certain 'Panorama'-style documentaries and radio's 'The Today Programme', 'The World This Weekend' and 'Today in Parliament' are all examples of potentially very useful programmes to help you build up a thorough knowledge of current events. Also regularly visit the legal websites mentioned in 'Useful addresses'.

Knowledge of the structure of the legal and judicial systems is vital. You should know who the Lord Chief Justice is, who the Director of Public Prosecutions is and what he or she does. You should be aware of recent controversial legal decisions, who took them and what their consequences are or could be. Who is the Home Secretary and why is he or she important? What do you think should be happening in the prison system at the moment? What reforms would you like to see implemented in the running of the police force?

THE INTERVIEW

Interviewers will ask questions with a view to being in a position to form an opinion about the quality of your thought and your ability to argue a particular case. You may be presented with a real or supposed set of circumstances and then be asked to comment on the legal implications of them. Is euthanasia wrong? What is the purpose of prison?

Recent events are very likely to form a large part of the interview. Ethical issues, political issues, police issues, prison reform issues – all of these are possible as the basis for questions at interview. An ability to see the opposite point of view while maintaining your own will mark you out as strong law degree material.

Don't forget that interview skills are greatly improved by practice. Chat through the issues we have discussed with your friends and then arrange for a teacher, careers officer or family friend to give you a mock interview.

THE INTERVIEW FOR WORK EXPERIENCE

Most of the above-mentioned tips would equally apply if you are going for an interview for work experience to a firm of solicitors or a set of chambers. However, in addition you may want to consider:

- Research the firm/chamber thoroughly before interview. Look at their brochure and website.
- Plan in advance what you think your key selling points are to the employer and make sure you find an opportunity in the interview to get your points across.
- Prepare a few questions to ask your interviewer about the firm at the end. You can demonstrate your preparation here by asking them about something you have read about the firm/chambers recently, if appropriate.
- Dress smartly and appropriately. Lawyers tend to look quite formal.
- Remember a nice firm confident handshake at the beginning and end of the interview.

POSSIBLE INTERVIEW QUESTIONS

Questions may be straightforward and specific, but they can range to the vague and border on the seemingly irrelevant. Be prepared for more than the blindingly obvious, 'Why do you want to study law?' question. But remember you wouldn't have been invited for interview unless you were a serious candidate for a place ... so be confident and let your talents shine through!

- Have you spoken to any lawyers about their work? Have you visited any courts?
- What makes a good judge/barrister/solicitor?
- What area of law are you interested in?
- What is the difference between the Law of Contract and the Law of Tort?
- Have you read about any cases recently?
- Should cannabis/euthanasia be legalised?
- What are the pros and cons of fusing the two branches of the legal profession?
- Should the police in this country be armed?
- If you were in a position of power, would you change the current civil legal aid situation?
- Should the police spend their time enforcing the laws concerned with begging?
- Why are some juvenile offenders 'sent on holiday'?
- What are your views on the handling of the Stephen Lawrence case?
- Should Britain or any other country be intervening in situations like Kosovo or Afghanistan?
- What are your views on the right to silence?
- How can you quantify compensation for victims of crime?
- Should criminals be allowed to sell their stories as 'exclusives'?
- Is it 'barbaric' to cane someone for vandalising cars?
- How does the law affect your daily life?
- What would happen if there were no law?
- Is it really necessary for the law to be entrenched in archaic tradition, ritual and jargon?
- How are law and morality related?
- Do you believe that all people have equal access to justice?
- What is justice?
- Why do we send criminals to prison? What are the alternatives?
- Should the media be more careful with the way in which they report real crime?

- Is law the best way to handle situations like domestic violence/child abuse/rape?
- Should British law encompass the laws of ethnic minorities since this society is so multi-cultural?
- What in your opinion are the causes of the increased crime rate?
- Should trial by jury be more or less common?
- Do you think capital punishment should be reinstated?
- Would the law in this country be any different if there was no Royal family?
- You are driving along a busy road with the window down, when a swarm of bees flies into your car. You panic and lose control of the car causing a huge pile-up. Are you legally responsible?
- A blind person, travelling by train, gets out at his/her destination. Unfortunately the platform is shorter than the train, and the blind person falls on to the ground, sustaining several injuries. Who, if anyone, can compensate him/her?

THE ENGLISH LEGAL SYSTEM

THE COURT STRUCTURE

The court structure is divided into two systems, those courts with civil jurisdiction and those with criminal jurisdiction.

Most cases are heard, in the first instance, by the County Court, but in cases where large amounts are in dispute, they will initially be heard in the High Court. Appeal from both the County Courts and the High Court is to the Court of Appeal (Civil Division).

All minor criminal matters are dealt with by the Magistrates Court. Serious cases are referred to the Crown Court. Here, the case will be decided upon by a lay jury, the essential element of the Common Law system. Cases can be appealed from the Magistrates Court to the Crown Court and from there to the Court of Appeal (Criminal Division).

The highest court in the land, not only for England and Wales, but also for Scotland and Northern Ireland, is the House of Lords, which only considers appeals in points of law. Each case is normally heard by five Law Lords in committee.

When a court is considering a European Community law point it may refer to the European Court of Justice in Luxembourg for interpretation.

JUDGES

By contrast with many other European countries, the judiciary in England and Wales is not a separate career. Judges are appointed from both branches of the legal profession. They serve in the House of Lords, the Court of Appeal, the High Court and Crown Court or as Circuit or District Judges.

The Circuit Judges sit either in Crown Courts to try criminal cases or in County Courts to try civil cases. District Judges sit in County Courts.

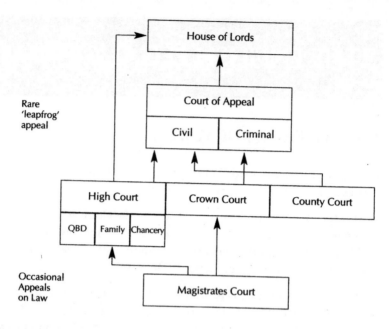

Outline of court structure

There are also part-time Judges appointed from both branches of the practising legal profession, who serve in the Crown Court, County Court or on various tribunals, for instance those dealing with unfair dismissal from employment.

In fact, most cases are dealt with not by Judges but by lay people, who are appointed to various tribunals because of their special knowledge, experience and good standing. For instance, the majority of minor criminal cases are judged by Justices of the Peace in Magistrates Courts. They are not legally qualified or paid but are respected members of the community who sit as magistrates part-time.

All members of the judiciary are appointed by the Lord Chancellor, who is a member of the Government and also speaker of the House of Lords. The Lord Chancellor holds a function similar to that of a Minister of Justice, although some matters concerning the administration of justice are the responsibility of the Home Secretary.

Once appointed, Judges are completely independent of both the legislature and the executive, and so are free to administer justice without fear of political interference.

TRIBUNALS

A system of Tribunals operates alongside the court system. Each type of Tribunal specialises in certain types of cases. Almost all Tribunals have been created by statute. For example, Employment Tribunals handle disputes and all aspects of work-related incidents. This includes disputed deductions from wages, unfair dismissal, redundancy, and discrimination. An Employment Tribunal is a more informal setting. There are no judges. Tribunals are headed by a Chairman who is appointed by the Lord Chancellor from a list of suitable applicants drawn up by the Independent Tribunal Service. In Employment Tribunals, for example, a Chairman will be assisted by two lay members. There is no standard form of procedure. Nonetheless, they operate in a similar way to court proceedings with witnesses usually giving evidence on oath.

THE WOOLF REFORMS

The Civil Justice System has always been seen as too expensive and too complex with long delays which led to the recent radical reform of civil procedure by the Civil Procedure Rules 1998 following the recommendations of Lord Woolf in 'Access to Justice', 1996, better known as *The Woolf Report*. Criminal procedure was put under similar radical scrutiny in 2000 by Auld Lord Justice. His report was published in 2001.

Background to the Woolf Reforms

Lord Woolf identified several problems with the system of civil justice. His criticisms of the old system were that it was:

- too expensive
- too slow
- too unequal – the rich litigant enjoyed an advantage over the underresourced litigant

- too uncertain – it was difficult to forecast the cost of civil litigation or how long it would take
- too complicated – it was incomprehensible to many litigants
- too fragmented in its organisation as no one had overall responsibility for its administration
- too adversarial as cases were run by the parties and not by the court.

He contrasted these criticisms with the principles which the Civil Justice System should attain in order to ensure access to justice. The attributes of his idealised Civil Justice System are that it should be:

- just in its result
- fair in the way it treats litigants
- efficient, in the sense that its procedures are appropriate and deliver justice at a suitable cost
- efficient, in the sense that the system is reasonably quick
- understandable to those who use it
- responsive to those who use it
- as certain in its outcome as is possible in a particular case
- effective, in the sense the system is adequately funded and organised.

The Civil Procedure Rules

The above principles have generated the Civil Procedure Rules ('the CPR Rules'). These rules are based on the draft rules prepared by Lord Woolf which were published simultaneously with his final report. They represent a radical shift in the way that civil litigation has been conducted since they came into force on 26th April 1999 and consequently in the working practices of practitioners.

The underlying aim of the CPR Rules are therefore to ensure that the civil justice system is accessible, fair and efficient. There is an overriding objective contained in the CPR Rules which enables the court to deal with a case justly by:

(a) ensuring that parties are on an equal footing
(b) saving expense
(c) dealing with the case in a way which is proportionate

- to the amount of money involved
- to the importance of the case

- to the complexity of the issues
- to the financial position of the parties

(d) ensuring that it is dealt with expeditiously and fairly
(e) allotting to it an appropriate share of the court's resources.

The court is under a duty to apply the overriding objective in interpreting the rules and in exercising its powers. The CPR Rules also set out pre-action protocols in respect of personal injury litigation and clinical disputes. These are statements of best practice in negotiating, encouraging exchange of information, and putting the parties in a position to settle fairly.

The Woolf Reforms also changed some legal terminology. For example a Plaintiff is now called a Claimant. It also changed the way in which proceedings may be started. It also imposed a duty on the court to manage cases in a particular way. For example, the duty now includes:

- encouraging parties to co-operate
- identifying issues at an early stage
- deciding promptly which issues can be deposed of summarily
- deciding the order of issues
- encouraging Alternative Dispute Resolution
- helping parties settle
- fixing a timetable
- considering costs benefit
- directing the trial process quickly and efficiently.

There are various sanctions for failing to comply with case management.

Claims are now allocated to one of three tracks: small claims, fast-track claims and multi-track claims.

1. Small claims track – this is most cases under £5,000.
2. Fast track cases – these are for claims between £5,000 and £15,000, although cases of this amount involving a complex point of law can be allocated to the multi-track.
3. Multi-track cases – these are claims over £15,000 or complex cases for less than this amount.

Comment on the post-Woolf Civil System

1. It is generally felt that the reforms are a qualified success.
2. The adversarial approach has been replaced by a moral co-operation between parties, and the use of ADR has increased.
3. The real issues of cases are being defined more quickly and this is leading to more cases ending in earlier settlements (rather than court door settlements on the day of trial).
4. The main problems are that:

   - the system is heavily front loaded, both in work to be done and in cost;
   - new procedures, such as pre-action protocols, allocation questionnaires and case management conferences are more complex;
   - the rules on time limits are not strictly enforced.

LEGAL TERMINOLOGY

ADMINISTRATIVE LAW: This is one of the core (or exemption) courses needed for a qualifying law degree. It usually teams up with Constitutional Law. It looks at the legal position of the government, public and local authorities and others who wield some kind of power over broadly defined policy, such as town planning and public health.

BLACK LETTER LAW: Means the fundamental areas of law like Law of Contract and Equity and Trusts. Doesn't include the more obscure or ephemeral law courses such as Feminist Perspectives in Law or Philosophy of Law. Tends only to examine law found in the law reports and statute books.

CIVIL LAW: Unfortunately has several meanings. Can refer to Roman Law but it is more likely to mean either, (a) Private Law i.e. all law other than Criminal, Administrative, Military and Church Law, or (b) the system of law which grew from Roman Law as opposed to the English system of Common Law.

CLINICAL LEGAL EDUCATION: This is the opportunity for you to get some hands-on experience with real life cases without being able to go hideously wrong. Students, under supervision from qualified practitioners, give free legal advice to clients and usually see a case right through from beginning to end.

COMMON LAW: This started about a thousand years ago in Britain. Up until then, each locality had its own customs and practices for dealing with problems and misdemeanours. So, Common Law was an attempt to iron out inconsistencies between different areas (basically so the men at the top could ensure their incomes and maintain their power) by applying one set of rules to similar circumstances.

COMMON PROFESSIONAL EXAMINATION (CPE): This is the one-year course that non-law graduates must take to get on to the Legal Practice Course, on the road to becoming a solicitor. The fees alone are over £4,000. You can avoid it by making sure you fit all the six core courses into your law degree.

CONSTITUTIONAL LAW: The rules that control what the Crown, judiciary, Parliament and government do in relation to the country and all the individuals within it. But the Constitution of the UK remains largely unwritten, unlike most other states and comprises statutes, Common Law rules and Constitutional Conventions.

CONTRACT LAW (LAW OF CONTRACT): There is an area of overlap between the Laws of Tort and Contract. The same set of circumstances can even lead to tortious or contractual actions, so look up Tort as well. Also, get used to this sort of far-fetched question: Adam has a TV which he promises to sell to Brian. Before he gets the telly though, Brian arranges to sell it to Chris for a tidy profit. But Adam changes his mind about the deal and sells it to David instead. When David receives the TV, it has badly damaged in transit so he calls Adam to complain. Adam directs David to the small print at the bottom of the receipt that passes all responsibility onto the haulier, and so on… Who owns the TV and who should pay for the repairs? Yes, this is the kind of thing that tutors dream up to antagonise their students. It is an example of the Law covering contracts i.e. legally binding agreements (written, verbal or even implied) between two or more parties coming about as a result of offer and acceptance although there are several other criteria that must be fulfilled too.

CORE SUBJECTS: Currently these are Constitutional and Administrative Law; Contract and Tort; Criminal Law; Equity and

Trusts, the Law of the EC and Property Law. They make up a qualifying law degree that will exempt you from the CPE course after you graduate.

CPE: See Common Professional Examination.

CPS: See Crown Prosecution Service.

CRIMINAL LAW: One of the cores. Crime is so often sensationalised that Criminal Law needs little introduction, but a lot of explanation, since the media continually obscure the legal points with hype. The Law basically defines those acts that are seen to be public wrongs and are therefore punishable by the state. Most crimes are made up of two elements – the act itself (actus reus) and the thinking behind it (the mens rea), both of which must be proved 'beyond reasonable doubt' in court to establish guilt.

CROWN PROSECUTION SERVICE (CPS): Born in 1986, the CPS, headed by the Director of Public Prosecutions, is responsible for virtually all the criminal proceedings brought by the police in England and Wales, although the lawyers within the CPS don't always bring a case to court.

DELICT (LAW OF DELICT): Simply the Scottish name for Tort.

DPP: Director of Public Prosecutions. See Crown Prosecution Service.

EC: European Community.

EQUITY: Half of the double act Equity and Trusts and one of the exemption courses. It is a (still developing) body of legal principles. It originated in the Middle Ages when, if you felt the Common Law was letting you down, you could petition the king's Chancellor for a fair appraisal of the situation. The Chancellor was keen to see justice done and wasn't too bothered about the rigidity of the Law. Even now, Equity prevails over the rules of Law, but the system of Equity is no longer as arbitrary as before. The main areas of Equity cover trusts, property and remedies (e.g. injunctions). Look up the 'Anton Piller' order that is a more recent example of Equity at work.

EVIDENCE: Remember that Tom Hanks film where the plot hinges on whether or not it's OK to use a crucial piece of evidence in court? Well, he lied in 'The Bonfire of the Vanities', and it was the Law of Evidence that he broke. This Law covers the presentation of facts and proof in court. It is often associated with hearsay evidence that isn't always admissible, but also covers topics like confessions and the credibility of witnesses.

EXEMPTION SUBJECTS: See Core Subjects.

JURISPRUDENCE: This is essentially the philosophy and theories of Law. Jurisprudence units get right down to grass roots level and usually examine Law from a number of angles, such as Natural Law, Marxism and the Critical School.

JUSTIS: This is a legal database giving you access to Law-related information on computer. It is very similar to Lexis and Lawtel.

LAND LAW (PROPERTY LAW): No points for guessing that this looks at who has rights (equitable and real) in different types of property and how these rights or responsibilities may be established or transferred. It covers subjects like mortgages, trusts, landlords and tenants, leases, easements and covenants.

LAW SCHOOL: Simply refers to the Law Departments within universities. Not to be confused with College of Law where students study their LPC.

LAWTEL: See Justis.

LEXIS: See Justis.

LPC: Legal Practice Course – the vocational one-year course after graduation (with a qualifying degree) and prior to the two-year training contract, designed for intending solicitors.

MOOT: This is a mock court room trial. Some universities have specially made rooms for that really authentic feel, and others even go as far as to include video cameras to record your performance! But on the whole, moots are organised as extra-curricular/optional activities to improve your confidence and help develop your legal skills of presenting a clear, logical argument and questioning a witness.

OBLIGATIONS (LAW OF OBLIGATIONS): This is just another name for the Laws of Tort and Contract.

PRIVATE LAW: These are those bits of the Law that are concerned with the relations between individuals that really have nothing to do with the state, but that doesn't stop the state intervening in certain circumstances of course. The areas are Family Law, Property Law and Trusts, Contract and Tort.

PROPERTY LAW: See Land Law.

PUBLIC LAW: Sometimes this is the core course Constitutional and Administrative thinly disguised. Strictly speaking, Public Law also includes areas like Tax Law and Criminal Law since they too are concerned with the relationship between the state and its individuals.

STATUTE: A general word for a law passed by parliament.

STATUTE BOOK: The list of all statutes that are currently in force.

SUBSTANTIVE LAW: Virtually all universities put most of the emphasis on substantive Law at the undergraduate level. It is simply that huge part of the Law that deals with duties and rights and everything else that does not fall into the category of practice and procedure.

TORT: Imagine it's a hot August day. You're gasping for a drink so you go into a cafe with your friend who buys you a bottle of beer. As you refill your glass you spot something a little suspicious and on closer inspection realise it's the decomposed remains of a snail! Do you:

(a) Drink the beer?

(b) Tell your friend to ask for a refund?

(c) Kick up a real furore and bring an action in tort against the manufacturer for negligence in production causing you to suffer shock and an upset stomach?

If your name was Mrs Donoghue and the year was 1928 then you'd go for option (c) and win the case, marking a milestone for the tort of negligence in English Law! Tort is largely concerned with providing compensation for people who have been wronged and suffered personal injury or damage to their property through negligence, defamation, nuisance, intimidation etc.

TRAINING CONTRACT: The name given to the two years after an LPC when you train as a kind of apprentice solicitor. In some cases, you can reduce the time spent by completing work placements as part of an undergraduate degree, but even then the training contract will last a minimum of one and a half years.

TRUSTS: See Equity. Taking the simplistic approach, trusts arise when someone transfers property to you but you can't use it. This is because the property is held on your behalf by trustees until you're 18. The property is entrusted to these trustees until you are able to choose to dissolve the trust and look after – or spend – the property yourself.

USEFUL ADDRESSES

USEFUL ADDRESSES

Solicitors

Institute of Legal Executives
Kempston Manor
Kempston
Bedford MK42 7AB
Tel: 01234 841000
www.ilex.org.uk

The Law Society
50–52 Chancery Lane
London WC2A 1SX
Tel: 020 7242 1222
www.lawsociety.org.uk

The Law Society of Northern Ireland
98 Victoria Street
Belfast BT1 3JZ
Tel: 02890 231614

The Law Society of Scotland
26 Drumsheugh Gardens
Edinburgh EH3 7YR
Tel: 0131 226 7411
www.lawscot.org.uk

Barristers

The General Council of the Bar
3 Bedford Row
London WC1R 4DB
Tel: 020 7242 0082
www.barcouncil.org.uk

The Education & Training Officer
The General Council of the Bar
2/3 Cursitor Street
London EC4A 1NE
Tel: 020 7440 4000

The Faculty of Advocates
Advocates Library
Parliament House
Edinburgh EH1 1RF
Tel: 0131 226 5071

Inns of Court
Gray's Inn
London WC1R 5EG
Tel: 020 7458 7900

The Inner Temple
London EC4Y

Tel: 020 7797 8250
www.innertemple.org.uk

The Middle Temple
London EC4Y 9AT
Tel: 020 7427 4800

Lincoln's Inn
London WC2A 3TL
Tel: 020 7405 0138
www.lincolnsinn.org.uk

General

Legal Action Group
242 Pentonville Road
London N1 9UW

Crown Prosecution Service
Personnel Branch
50 Ludgate Hill
London EC4M 7EX
Tel: 020 7796 8500
www.cps.gov.uk

Institute of Professional Legal Studies
10 Lennox Vale
Malone Road
Belfast
Tel: 02890 245133
www.qub.ac.uk/ipls

USEFUL BOOKS

There are a vast number of books written about the law and the legal profession and new ones are constantly being published. It is worth a trip to your school library, your local public library and your careers office to check what is available. Here are some we think might be useful to you.

The legal profession

Ivanhoe Career Guide to the Legal Profession, Cambridge Market Intelligence. An overview of the legal profession
Legal Profession, CSU. The options from graduation to qualification
GTI Law Journal, GTI. Practical information about life as a solicitor or barrister, written by practitioners

Law Casebook, Hobsons. An overview of career options in law
Career Opportunities in the International Legal Field, The Law Society.
  Opportunities for qualified lawyers and law graduates worldwide
Solicitors' & Barristers' National Directory, The Law Society.
Chambers & Partners Directory of the Legal Profession, Chambers &
  Partners Publishing. A comprehensive directory of firms of solicitors
  and barristers' chambers
The Legal 500 by John Pritchard, Legalease. A detailed account of the
  UK legal profession
Solicitors' Regional Directory – Your Guide to Choosing a Solicitor, The
  Law Society. A list of every firm in practice by region and town
The Guide to Work Experience for Intending Lawyers, GTI. Information
  on getting vacation placements and mini-pupillages
The Bar Directory, FT Law & Tax. Details of chambers and barristers
Chambers Pupillages & Awards Handbook, GTI. Details of chambers in
  England and Wales offering pupillages
Prospects Legal, Central Services Unit.

General Books on Higher Education

Degree Course Offers, Brian Heap, Trotman.
Directory of University and College Entry, Trotman.
Disabled Students' Guide to University, Trotman.
Entrance Guide to Higher Education in Scotland, Committee of Scottish
  Higher Education Principals.
Getting into Oxford and Cambridge, Trotman.
Choosing Your Degree Course and University, Brian Heap, Trotman.
How to Complete Your UCAS Form, Tony Higgins, Trotman.
Student Book, Klaus Boehm and Jenny Lees-Spalding (editors), Trotman.
Students' Money Matters, Trotman.
UCAS Handbook, UCAS.
University and College Entrance – the Official Guide, UCAS.

General books on law

There are a number of good introductory texts on English Law and the
processes of learning the law. Among the ones we would recommend are:

An Introduction to Law, 4th edition, P. Harris, Butterworths.
Learning Legal Rules, 3rd edition, J.A. Holland & J.S. Webb, Blackstone
    Press.
Learning Legal Skills, S. Lee & M. Fox, Blackstone Press.

Miscarriages of justice and the legal system
Blind Justice, John Eddleston, ABC-CLIO.
The Law Machine, Marcel Berlins and Clare Dyer, Penguin.
More Rough Justice, P. Hill & M. Young, Penguin.
Presumed Guilty: The British Legal System Exposed,M. Mansfield,
    Heinemann.
Standing Accused, M. McConville et al, Clarendon Press.
Report of the Royal Commission on Criminal Justice, Runciman
    Commission, HMSO, 1993.
Justice in Error,C. Walker & K. Starmer (eds), Blackstone Press.

Trial by Jury
Jury Trial, J. Baldwin & M. McConville, Oxford University Press.
Justice in Error, C. Walker & K. Starmer (eds), Blackstone Press.
A Matter of Justice, M. Zander, Oxford University Press.

Civil Legal Aid
Smith & Bailey on the Modern English Legal System, S.H. Bailey & M.J.
    Gunn, Sweet & Maxwell, 1991.
Achieving Civil Justice, R. Smith (ed), Legal Action Group.
Tomorrow's Lawyers, P.A. Thomas (ed), Blackwell.

Professional Journals

Commercial Lawyer: A monthly magazine
The Lawyer: A weekly newspaper for solicitors and barristers. www.the-
    lawyer.co.uk
The Law Society Gazette: Available from the Law Society
Legal Business: Available from Legalease
Legal Action: Bulletin of the Legal Action Group
The Economist

National Press

The Times (Tuesday), *The Independent* (Wednesday)

USEFUL LEGAL WEBSITES

Note that addresses may change.

The College of Law
www.lawcol.org.uk
GTI – publishers of legal publications
www.gti.co.uk
Legalease – legal publishers
www.legalease.co.uk
Butterworths – legal publishers
www.butterworths.co.uk
Information for Lawyers – a vast selection of links and information
www.infolaw.co.uk
On-line Law – a huge database of information on firms and chambers
www.online-law.co.uk
Prospects Legal
www.prospects.csu.ac.uk
Advice for CPE and LPC applicants
www.lawcabs.ac.uk
Directory of law firms and chambers
www.chambersandpartners.com
Law careers
www.lawcareers.net
On-line pupillage application system
www.olpas.co.uk